UNDERSTANDING
WIDOWS,
VICTIMS OF ADULTERY,
AND *DIVORCE*

Barb Neff

ISBN 978-1-63961-416-5 (paperback)
ISBN 978-1-63961-417-2 (digital)

Copyright © 2022 by Barb Neff

All rights reserved. No part of this publication may be reproduced, distributed, or transmitted in any form or by any means, including photocopying, recording, or other electronic or mechanical methods without the prior written permission of the publisher. For permission requests, solicit the publisher via the address below.

Christian Faith Publishing
832 Park Avenue
Meadville, PA 16335
www.christianfaithpublishing.com

All biblical citations were taken from the New King James Version unless otherwise stated.

Printed in the United States of America

Contents

Acknowledgments 5
Introduction..7
Chapter 1: How It All Began 9
Chapter 2: The Three Separations 21
Chapter 3: Who Is This About? 50
Chapter 4: How Does God Feel About Us?.............58
Chapter 5: What Made Us Who We Are? 75
Chapter 6: Our Defining Hope! 103

Acknowledgments

Thanks to God, Jesus, and the Holy Spirit for seeing me through each phase of writing this. I love them dearly for their mercy and grace shown to me.

I appreciate my family for their understanding and patience while I was working on the book. I love them dearly and appreciate all the help they have given me as a widow.

Thanks to Pastor Rick Collens for his help and encouragement toward my growth in the Lord.

Thanks to my Dr. Eric Gertner for his encouragement in my writing. It touched me deeply since he is Jewish and I had his blessing on my writing project. This means so much to me.

Thanks to my neighbor Cathy Bendel for her constant encouragement. Cathy has a good heart, and she has helped me when I was ill. Her nursing skills were helpful in keeping me going so I could complete what God put on my heart.

I am grateful to my church family. To the different churches I have attended, you are all precious to me, and I love you dearly.

I have deep gratitude for my current church family for all they did to help me, mostly the Bible studies, to deepen my knowledge of all God has for us. A special appreciation to Pastor William Ritzenthaler for his diligence by having the Bible studies to help us grow in the Lord.

Introduction

As hard as it is to believe, I experienced all three—to be a victim of adultery, divorce, and widowhood with the same man. Until I started writing this book, my understanding of how much they were alike yet how differently each one could affect your life was minimal.

All this started over fifty years ago. I never thought of checking out what happened, why I responded the way I did, or what effect each one had on me.

Writing this book was put on my heart years before I knew the subject.

As far as training, I completed one-year training at Word of Faith, Leadership and Bible Institute. God's leading, my training, and my experiences have helped me to write this to help others understand what they are going through during these trying experiences.

Chapter 1

How It All Began

God put in my heart that I was going to write a book over eight and a half years ago. However, I was unaware of the topic or the title. The thing was, my husband was still alive at that time, and this subject would have been in an unknown territory for me. I always kept this in the back of my mind—watching for what I could write about while waiting for the Lord's leading and direction.

Patiently watching and waiting for some topic I knew about and could share with others that would be relevant for them, I created a file called "Future Book" and was packing it with things I thought would be of help but what did I know. I knew that since it was from Him, He would be with me to teach and guide me in the way I should go.

> *I will instruct you and teach you in the way you should go; I will guide you with My eye.* (Psalm 32–8)

Three years after my husband passed away, the subject of the book began to come to life. This was when I started working with widows but, at that time, was unaware that this was to be the subject of the book. Maybe I was just slow, but one day, I realized that the Lord was putting the widow in my path and leading me to write about them. Each widow came into my life one at a time. As I realized that the widows were the assignments God put on my heart, I knew that this was the subject of the book.

After working with the widows and gaining insight for three and a half years was when I finally started to put life into writing this.

I started making friends with widows. At first, it was just friendship. However, the number of widows I visited kept increasing. I would bake and take some baked goods to them and spend some time with them—mostly helping them reflect on the good times they had. Sometimes, I prayed with them if I felt it was needed. I especially visited those who were unable to drive anymore and had no way of getting out to others. Even though I did not know this was what God wanted me to write about, I was getting a better understanding of widows. I realized that this was what God wanted me to write about. Now, I understood my desire to visit and learn from the widows. He had His hand in it all along. Thus, researching widows in the Bible had a strong pull on me after having hands-on experience.

This became my outlet instead of just sitting and trying to figure out what to do next. This was how I could help in little ways to make the lives of others a little better. Guess what? It was also helping me with a reason to get out and do something for others. Taking that first step, I got to know all these wonderful widows.

There is a lot I do not know. I am just sharing what I learned by observation and doing something.

Many scriptures will be used throughout the book to show God knows our human issues. This is why the Bible is referred to as our user's manual. Although this was written for women, without men, women would not be in one of these positions. Men should read this because they will not only find some scriptural principles they can use but also have more insight into women in their lives. This will help the men to understand widows and victims of adultery and divorce so they will know how to deal with any that occurred in their lives.

I like the saying, "Get up, get dressed, get going!" That is what we should think about every day. I know some of us are older with aches and pains, but it seems they fade into nothingness if your mind is set on doing good things to help others. In plain words, you just need something to do. Talk to God and ask Him to help you to use your strength and talents to help in the direction you should go. What do you like doing? Find out who you can share them with. This is all up to you!

In all your ways acknowledge Him, and
He shall direct your path. (Proverbs 3:6)

God has a plan for your life. Your spouse did not define you. He was an extension of who you are. This is your beginning. It is not the end of your life!

When I started writing, I never thought of putting in victims of adultery and divorce. However, the more I studied the Bible, I came to understand that they had direct ties to the subject of spouse separation and had to be included.

In the beginning, I was only going to write about widows, but the more I looked at the widows, victims of adultery, and divorces and the similarities of what they went through, I knew they had to be together. God showed me, as I researched, that they belonged together. The more I looked at it, I was confident I was on the right track with where I was being directed when I saw a scripture where God had the two of them together—widows and divorced (victims of adultery wasn't mentioned). It also shows how the father or husband approves or overrules what you vow because they are your head covering.

> *If a man makes a vow to the Lord, or swears an oath to bind himself by some agreement, he shall not break his word; he shall do according to all that proceeds out of his mouth.* (Numbers 30:2)

> *Or if a woman makes a vow to the Lord and binds herself by some agreement while in her father's house in her youth.* (Numbers 30:3)

> *Also, any vow of a widow or a divorced woman, by which she has bound herself, shall stand against her. If she vowed in her*

> *husband's house, or bound herself with an agreement or an oath, and her husband heard it and made no response to her and did not overrule her, then all her vows shall stand, and any agreement by which she bound herself shall stand.* (Numbers 30:9–11)

> *Every vow and every binding oath to afflict her soul, her husband may confirm it, or her husband may make it void.* (Numbers 30:13)

This shows that a vow by a man is binding because he is considered the head of the family. I had initially considered including men, even though this was mostly directed toward women. I realized that men feel the same trauma as women do! The biggest one for men is feeling left out because they are looked at as the stronger one. We women know better—let them get a cold and they are dying! But trauma is trauma. Strength has nothing to do with how you feel at these times. Also, they were the breadwinners and are, therefore, unable to be around the kids as much as their partner can, so the daily contact to the children isn't as close to the father as the mother. As far as the word *widower*, it is not found anywhere in the Scripture. Why? Because man was made first and considered the head of the family. The man is the protector and gave stability to the family unit. They can use this same information for themselves, even though I will be mostly talking about women.

Just so you know, even though I love to write, I make no claims to be a writer.

As I started to write, I knew it was a leading of the Lord, as He kept me going and I relied heavily upon Him for His encouragement and direction. I was apprehensive and uncertain at first but trusted God.

> *Study to show thyself approved unto God, a workman that needs not be ashamed, rightly dividing the word of truth.* (2 Timothy 2:15)

Continuous study and searching of this subject for over that last three and a half years have been extremely interesting and rewarding. I was not only studying the Bible but also studying what I did at each phase of the *Understanding Widows, Victims of Adultery, and Divorce*. I learned a lot about what the Bible said about widows, but I also learned a lot about myself and what kind of person I really was deep down inside.

Now, I will admit that because of my age—seventy-nine—my memory is not as sharp as it was when all these things happened, but I will do the best I can with the things I remember going through at that time. When looking for answers in the Bible—yes, I do still need this, especially when I want to find out about something—I use all the tools necessary to see what God has waiting for me. The Bible is my treasure chest! I am enjoying the internet and how much you can glean from it. It helps you when you want better insight into something, especially if you want a greater understanding of what you are researching.

Why am I writing about this? The answer is—I am one of you. I have been widowed for eight years. Because of adultery, I divorced my husband for three years, whom I remarried, so I have experience in all three categories. I will be taking you through some of the things that you will encounter and was unprepared for and will be including things that I have learned in over fifty years.

Now, that explains how this book began, but for the book's purpose, we need to know how the first man/woman's experience began—this first and best example of how God started what we now know as providing a soul mate and why we took our marriage vow to have our spouse as our soul mate.

> *And then the Lord said, "It is not good that man should be alone; I will make him a helper comparable to him." (Genesis 2:18)*

> *And Adam gave names to all cattle, to the birds of the air, and to every beast of the field. But for Adam there was not found a helper comparable to him. And the Lord God caused a deep sleep to fall on Adam, and he slept: and He took one of his ribs; and closed up the flesh in its place. And the rib which the Lord God had taken from man, He made a woman, and brought her to the man. And Adam said, "This is now*

bone of my bones, and flesh of my flesh: She shall be called Woman because she was taken out of Man." Therefore, a man shall leave his father and mother and be joined to his wife and they shall become one flesh. And they were both naked, the man and his wife, and were not ashamed. (Genesis 2:20–25)

That was the original happening of "Man Meets Woman!"

Here is a little synopsis of our beginning since there was only one Adam and Eve, and ours didn't quite happen that way.

When you have your first encounter with your potential husband—your first encounter is when you first see him and you have a warm feeling in your heart—you'd hope he is as interested in you as you are in him. Then he looks at you and starts to talk, and you know right away that this is a person of special interest. You have your dating time, and while getting to know him and deep down you know he is the one that will become your soul mate, he feels the same way, and after a period of courtship, you are wed. You are no longer alone. The two of you have become one.

You lived your lives together and the years fly by. When unexpectedly, it happens—the oneness is broken. You lost your spouse in one of three ways—widowed, victim of adultery, or divorced.

And now, this is the beginning of your life without your spouse. This is how this new chapter in your life began. This is our beginning—for us to be at the spot we are in right now because of the loss of our significant other. Each one of our beginnings may differ in many ways, but when you become a *widow,* a victim of adultery, or divorced, you'll be looking for something that will help you cope with the new place in life that has been dealt to you and to move forward. Because of this, you are on the verge of a new beginning—how you become the person you were meant to be regardless of what happened to your life. How you move into your new life depends on how much you do not want to remain at the spot you are at. It's time to look forward to the new life ahead.

I hope that as you read this book, you will find some encouragement and insight that can help you become a stronger, more independent, and self-reliant woman. And that you know there is hope and a fulfilling future after any one of these occurrences happen in your life.

Since this is about widows—occurrences which I wanted to call infidelity but are really victims of adultery and divorce—the occurrence that we experience first is our beginning into being without our spouse. It is where our lives have changed forever. (Please keep your situation in mind as we cover each one of the three of them so you can see why you reacted differently than others who had these experiences. Everyone does not react in the same way you do, so make no expectation of others.) We need to go to the point wherein one of these three came first in your life. We can have any one, two, or all three of these happen in our lives. However, the defining one is the first one you have experienced. This will determine how you react if you do have one of the others happen to you in your life at another time.

Just so you understand, here is my short definition for widow and victim of adultery and divorce.

A *widow* is a woman who was married when her spouse died. A *victim of adultery* is when your partner is having sex while they are committed to you but with someone other than you. A *divorced man/woman* is a married person who are separated from their spouse because of deciding to divorce instead of remaining in the marriage. We must also consider couples in fornication, sometimes with children, that separate. All these will be covered more completely and with more detail later in the book. This is just a quick reference for right now.

We immediately think about death as the extreme separation of a husband and wife. Everywhere I looked on the internet, all the experts say the same thing, so they must be right, right? I have a different understanding I will be sharing in the next chapter under the section on widows. You must see the explanation no one else has even considered.

However, when it comes to victim of adultery, the stress can be more extreme than widow separation. I have a different understanding that I will be sharing in the next chapter under "Victims of Adultery." You must see this explanation that no one else has even considered. In fact, victims of adultery were never given any consideration when talking about separations of your spouse. It will be included in this book.

With the *divorce*, you lost your spouse as well and can have the same trauma as death separation if you are the injured party—since they were your soul mate.

When I refer to widowed, victims of adultery, or divorced, you must also consider the split-ups of families where the couple never got married but were in fornication. They are being included in this since these separations can be traumatic also. All these different losses are to be looked at throughout the whole book.

No matter how you look at it, you are without your partner!

Our beginning may differ in many ways and, at the same time, may have many similarities. Of course we only have one beginning, and that is the first one you encounter. Any that occur after that would be the second, third, and could continue if you decide to remarry. It is possible for you to experience all three at one time or another in your lifetime—I have. Since there are three different things that could have happened to you—widowhood, victim of adultery, or divorce—should each have a different effect and solution? Of course! You are in a different spot and would react differently since you already had one trauma. The most important factor I cannot stress enough is how we deal with the first trauma because it is a stepping-stone to any other trauma we may experience! However, the main thing that makes each experience the same is that you have been separated from your spouse. The oneness is broken—*whether it is by widowhood*, which we think of as one of the hardest separations, *or by being a victim of adultery*, a separation of ultimate betrayal! *Or by divorce*, which is the only one that happens sometimes as a separation by mutual agreement, or *by couples in fornication who separate*, which needs consideration also.

Since you no longer have the love in your heart, you eagerly desire again. Now would be the perfect time to look to God. If you have already made your commitment to Him. You have an advocate already. This relationship with God is the one thing you can count on. He will never leave you like the love of your earthly spouse has. This is a spiritual oneness.

> *But he who is joined to the Lord is one spirit with Him.* (1 Corinthians 6:17)

Chapter 2

The Three Separations

Death Separation—Widowhood

A widow had to be a married woman whose husband has died and who remains unmarried. This is Old Testament definition. The Hebrew word translation for *widow* is *almanac*.

This separation is totally out of your control! There is the possibility that you can know it is coming if your husband has been ill, or it can be a very sudden loss because of an accident or by dying in sleep without illness. No matter how you look at it, death loss is traumatic!

Widowhood is considered by experts to be the number one stressor for you. (I will quote this later in the chapter to verify this fact.)

However, I tend to disagree with this theory.

- *First*—because your spouse leaving you was a natural occurrence of life. We should not have been surprised about it. Maybe the time it happened was unexpected, but we all know that this is the cycle of life. We are not considering all the full facts at that time because our love for our spouse blinds us to it. Don't take it personal.
- *Second*—it was his time to go home to God. His leaving had nothing to do with you.
- *Third*—you are taking it personal. He did nothing to you. Your loss has blinded you to truths and facts about death and your loss of having your spouse with you. It is the natural order of life.

I know this sounds cruel, but if you really look at it, it is factual!

> *For the living know they will die.* (Ecclesiastes 9:5)

If this is the first separation you have, you will be more prone to have *grief* than if a victim of adultery or divorce were the first separation you experience.

> *Blessed are they that mourn, for they shall be comforted.* (Matthew 5:4)

Many of you were never separated from your spouse before. This being your first separation from your spouse is an extremely difficult spot to be in because no matter how we prepare, we are unprepared!

EMOTIONAL STAGES OF WIDOWHOOD

1. At first, you felt *shocked* and was unaware of what to do or where to turn and were almost comatose.
2. Then comes *disbelief.* You can't believe this happened.
3. *Numbness* sets in, and you are not sure which way to turn.
4. You become *angry* that this happened to you.
5. Finally, you have no choice but to *accept* what has happened.

The two of you were one. You worked together, laughed together, enjoyed one another, and loved each other. You were fulfilled within your relationship with each other.

What happened was that the oneness is broken by no fault of your own because the person, who was your other half and made you whole, is gone.

Suddenly, you are like a duck out of water—looking for direction with no help in sight. You get all the clichés. "Let me know if you need anything." Of course you do. You cannot get anyone to really commit to anything concrete though. Another one is, "I'll be there for you," or "I am only a phone call away." Another good one is, "I understand!" I cringe when I hear someone say that—because no one can really understand your situation and how you feel or are dealing with it. When someone says, "I understand," you get turned off because it does not mean a thing to you. They are wasting their breath. Everyone deals with things differently, so how can they understand?

At this time, please do not tell them how your spouse died. They do not want to hear it! It does not mean anything to them right now. It is just not the time for this type of discussion.

Then when the first night comes around and everyone goes home, this is when the loneliness finally sets in. What you missed most was the pillow talk. This was the time when you went to bed and you spent uninterrupted time together without any of life's distractions. You probably started by discussing the things that happened that day, proceeding to share what bothers both of you and things that went wrong for you. You then got more personal and shared your emotional wants, needs, feelings, and intimacy.

No matter how you look at it, you will forever be without your partner the rest of your life. You need to face that! Your usual household routine is not the only thing you will be doing. Now, you have your spouse's responsibilities to also take care of.

The spot you are in that first day, with the empty pit in your stomach—you are unable to even think about what you need the next minute, let alone what you need to exist! Now is the time when you need to be careful that your mind does not keep replaying this event day and night. You could wind up in grief. Because if you remain in the trauma state too long, it turns into grief. Find something to do outside of your home. You have three of the best to help you out; God is there all the time to hear your prayers. Jesus is interceding for you, and the Holy Spirit is you helper.

What is the difference between mourning and grief?

- Mourning is external. *Mourning* is the shared social response to loss.
- Grief is internal. The term *grief* refers to our thoughts and feeling on the inside.

Some get so traumatized from their grief that they get broken heart syndrome. What is it? It is a temporary heart condition often brought on by stressful situations and extreme emotions. It may also be called stress cardiomyopathy and takotsubo cardiomyopathy. That is why I expressed not to let your trauma go into grief because of this factor.

He heals the brokenhearted and binds up their wounds. (Psalms 147:3)

Not everyone grieves but realize that you need to go on. For those that grieve, there are plenty of good places you can look for help. I know that the Methodist church has a program called "Grief Share," which I heard can be helpful for grief, also for grief other than spousal.

Somehow, you manage to pull yourself together enough and begin some of the things you usually do every day—things that you tend to do automatically, like take a bath, brush your teeth, and eat. These are easy!

You are doing a lot of thinking right now about how you are going to deal with all the necessary things. Must I sell the house? Do I have enough to get by financially? What is going to happen to me? Will I be able to manage on my own? Who can I depend on to help me if I need to? Who can I turn to when I need help with tasks that I am unable to do? Does the church have a program set up to help widows or that they can socialize with each other?

It is a scary spot to be in! You literally are facing everything alone! You may be blessed with people/family around to support you, but you *are* now on your own. Your attention will start, at some point, to go from looking back at what happened in the past, and you start to look ahead to where you are going from here.

> *But one thing I do, forgetting the things which are behind and reaching forward to the things which are ahead.* (Philippians 3:13)

A good reminder here is that your rearview mirror on the car is quite small. During operation of the car, it really is not necessary to look back that much. However, the windshield on the car is quite open and huge. Now you need to focus on looking ahead, just like you do when you are driving your car. Be focused on going forward because you are unable to go back at all.

> *"The past is your memories. The future is your life."*—Barb Neff

This is when you think of planning what you want to do with your life. You need to depend on all that is within you to make your transition go smoother. Just what do you have in you? What type of person would you define yourself as? What are your weaknesses and strengths? You need to know yourself better than you ever did before because your identity has changed. When you wed, your title was "married." You no longer have that identity but have a new identity! *Widow*!

Hopefully, you are getting ready to move on. Now would be a perfect time to look to God, Jesus, and the Holy Spirit to help you take the next steps in your life. Now would be the perfect time to have Jesus in your life. There is no need to be alone. Confessing your sins and asking for forgiveness is the first step. Then ask Jesus to come in your life, and He will. You have oneness again, but with Jesus, you are no longer alone. By inviting Jesus into your heart, you have a new identity. He came into your heart just like you and your spouse became one by letting your spouse in your heart. Jesus always loved you and always wanted to dwell in your heart. But for love to be complete, you must love Him as much as He loves you, in the same way you loved your spouse. The difference is that this is a spiritual oneness that you establish with the Lord. You can depend on Him to help you because, now, you have an advocate with Jesus in your heart! With God at your side, you can depend on Him to give you the peace you need at this time. You can count on Him all the time.

Start by reading your Bible. This is how God talks to you. You will need Psalms, at first, to get comfort and see

His face. By His face, you know who Jesus is, just like you can recognize someone by their face.

The time has come to make some choices. You can rely on God to direct you. Talk to Him daily—that's prayer. With God, you can have the pillow talk again at bedtime.

> *Be angry, and do not sin. Meditate within your heart on your bed and be still.* (Psalm 4:4)

> *When I remember you on my bed, I mediate on You in the night watches.* (Psalm 63:6)

What are my choices? Do I want to sit here and wallow in my loneliness and remain in the numb state or do something about it? You relied on your spouse to help you make decisions, but now, that is missing. Now you can rely on God to help you. In the beginning, it seems scary, but you can do whatever you imagine with God at your side.

> *I can do all things through Christ who strengthens me.* (Philippians 4:13)

Always, always, always remember you are *never* alone since God is in your heart and always there.

> *Be strong and of good courage, do not fear or be afraid of them; for the Lord your God, He is the One that goes with*

you. He will not leave you nor forsake you.
(Deuteronomy 31:6)

At this point, you are looking for something that would help you get though the transition to some normalcy in your life again.

Your New Normal

Your old normal has vanished forever! Caused by a deep tragic loss. You can find your new normal when you turn to the Lord and learn to lean on Him to lead you out of loss and into new life.

The poverty rate for widows is three to four times higher than elderly married women (Social Security Administration).

The death of a spouse is dealt with differently by each sex because of necessity or beliefs. Men need their helper back and tend to marry quickly after the death of their wife, some, as soon as three months. Women, on the other hand, do not feel the same urgency at first. They are busy addressing everything that needs their immediate attention. Eventually, the need for financial assistance makes them start looking for another partner. Their process is slower for them. Many times the elderly on social security live together—yes, fornication at their age. The reason they do not marry is because one of them will lose their social security benefits, and they need both to be able afford to pay the bills because they cannot make it financially on their own. It's a shame the government put them in a position that they are sinning against God. The older people who came from a poorer background didn't look that far ahead and didn't have the training on finances. The younger couples live together, in fornication, so they can pool their finances together to have a better lifestyle. Since they got together on a trial basis to see if they are compatible, they risk the chance of having children. Is this the pattern you want your children to replicate? Most times these trials do not last, and marriage, what the woman wanted, love and marriage, hardly ever does happen. What the man wanted are a helper and sex. The man gets what he is looking for, and the woman is stuck in a situation that is hard to get out of because most of the time there are children involved.

I know of a couple in my own family that lived together over twenty years with grown children who split up. This breaks the family unit apart. There are times that they will do it again, not learning a lesson from their first mistake. There is a problem with commitment on both parties involved because of fear of it failing; however, by doing it, they are setting themselves up for failure, again. Do the right thing! You know in your heart what it is.

VICTIMS OF ADULTERY SEPARATION

Adult comes from the Latin verb *adolescere*, which means "to grow up, mature." *Adultery*, on the other hand, is derived from the Old French word *avoutre*, which, in turn, evolved from distinct Latin verb *adulterare*, which means "to corrupt."

Bible meaning of adultery—according to *Easton's Bible Dictionary*, the simple meaning of *adultery* is "marital infidelity." An adulterer was a man who had illicit intercourse with a married or betrothed woman, and such a woman was an adulteress.

Infidelity is the breaking of a promise to remain faithful to a romantic partner—whether that promise was a part of marriage vows or a privately uttered agreement. Widowed and divorced have real identities. I am unable to find an identity for victims of adultery to attest to. That is what makes this one of the hardest because you are unable to find an identity. This is up to you to create who you really are and what core belief system will be your guiding light.

SOME NOTEWORTHY QUOTES BY WOODROW M. KROLL:

When adultery walks in, everything worth having walks out.

Adultery occurs in the head, long before it occurs in the bed.

Adultery is a moment of pleasure and a lifetime of pain. It's not worth it.

SOME SCRIPTURES ON ADULTERY:

Whoever commits adultery with a woman lacks understanding; he who does so destroys his own soul. (Proverbs 6:32)

> *But I say unto you whosoever looks on a woman to lusts for her has already committed adultery with her in his heart.* (Matthew 5:28)

The Bible is clear that adultery is sinful. Adultery is when the covenant of marriage is broken by fornication and lust. If you are married, you must not engage in any sexual relations with anyone who is not your spouse—if you do, that is adultery. Sexual relationships (in any form) must only be with your spouse. Period. Marriage is sacred—an institution designed by God. Marriage is not just a piece of paper. It is a covenant. So what does the Bible specifically say about adultery?

The sexual, immoral, and adulterous—it goes hand in hand. Sexual sins are specifically highlighted in Scripture and are set apart from other sins—because sexual sins are not just a sin against God but also against our own body.

> *Flee sexual immorality. Every sin that a man does is outside the body, but he who commits sexual immorality sins against his own body. Or do you not know that your body is the temple of the Holy Spirit who is in you, whom you have from God, and you are not your own?* (1 Corinthians 6:18–19)

The seventh commandment says:

> *You shall not commit adultery.* (Exodus 20:14)

This is much more than checking off a box on the rules list. Jesus is saying that lustful intent is the same thing as adultery. The physical act of adultery is just the external consummation of internal sin.

The sin always begins in the heart. No one just falls into sin—it is a slow, slippery decline into sin. Sin is always born in the depths of our wicked heart.

> *For out of the heart proceed evil thoughts, murders, adulteries, fornications, thefts, false witness, and blasphemies.* (Matthew 15:19)

Is adultery grounds for divorce?

God offers forgiveness and is eager and willing to forgive sinners who have repented. Adultery does not always mean that the marriage cannot be saved. Marriage was designed in the beginning to be permanent. (This is not talking about homes where one spouse is in danger from the violent abuse of another.) Is your home broken in by adultery? There is hope. Seek certified counselors in your area. They can help.

Emotional Stages of Victims of Adultery

1. *Shocked*—that he would do this to you. You may feel like you are going crazy and unable to hold it together. You go between despair that your marriage is over and hope that it will be restored. These feelings make it almost impossible to cope with daily routines.
2. *Denial*—that you can't believe that this is happening to you.
3. *Guilt*—because you feel as if you did something wrong for him to do this.
4. *Anger*—not just at him but for him letting this happen to ruin your lives together.
5. *Depression*—because you don't understand how you'll feel like you can be an acceptable person again.
6. *Acceptance*—of the situation so you can go on.

Adultery separation is not considered when looking at the separation from your spouse, like widowhood or divorce is. I am unaware of anyone who includes all three of them together when looking at the breaking of oneness in a marriage.

Adultery separation is the toughest one to experience, even more so if this is your first spouse separation. It has to do with the heartache of the betrayal. This is a willful act by the spouse to break the marriage vow that you both took together to become one before God.

This was my first spouse separation and was the least talked about. My understanding at the time I was going through this was, why was this so hard?

I think it's because you need to face him every day and find it hard to comprehend how he could do this to you. This is very personal.

Having experienced all three and if you would ask me which of the three separations I would list as the hardest one to go through, it would be victims of adultery. Here is why!

The one who cheated is still with you, but you and your spouse are no longer one. So you are facing daily trauma because you are facing the betrayal every day—and with many uncertainties that go with it, especially if you chose to stay when the first adultery happened. And it can happen again in your marriage.

If you know you are not strong enough, many choose to go—thus, divorce!

Here are some reasons you might choose to stay:

1. You are embarrassed, and you want to hide the affair.
2. You feel insecure to go out on your own.
3. You are more concerned of the family welfare than yourself.
4. You want to stay to help those who have an addiction (drugs, alcohol, gambling, or sex) because they made a mistake.

Sorry, but things are never going back to normal, not for you—*ever*, unless the addiction is dealt with! Alcohol, drugs, and gambling lead them to places they would not normally go. This is where they meet the savory people where the sex comes in. There are many programs out there to help you with these addictions if you want to pursue this path to stay with your spouse. The other addiction is sex—that is not usually considered or talked about much. This is the one that is hidden by the family. There are so many avenues for this one to run rampant because it can be started right in your home via the computer. This one is harder to deal with because all sex starts in the mind. The mind must be healed before this addiction can be dealt with.

Many women will stay over regular addictions because they are not personal. But with someone addicted to sex, this goes into a different category. It is harder to deal with because it is personal and deals with the heart. It is the very core of why you are together as a couple. He made the decision to separate by being unfaithful to you, which caused you pain. He is your head covering, and he betrayed the position he took when he wed you. He became your protector before God. He broke that vow.

You were hurt and hurt—deeply! The broken heart is unbearable at times. This goes to the deepest part of your soul.

My spirit is broken. (Job 17:1)

> *The spirit of a man will sustain him in sickness, but who can bear a broken spirit?* (Proverbs 18:14)

> *A merry heart makes a cheerful countenance, but by sorrow of the heart the spirit is broken.* (Proverbs 15:13)

Do you stick it out or run for the door? Unless they repent and are sorry and ask for forgiveness of what they did to you, it would be impossible to move on. It would always be in the back of your mind that they will do it again. You need to know that this can haunt you in an instant. (Satan is always ready to help, even for the rest of your life! Even after they passed, the hurt will still come back!) This battle is continual. Satan never lets you forget.

With sex addiction, it is not an only a onetime happening. You can be guaranteed it will happen again. My question to you is, how often in your lifetime can you bear that your heart can be broken again and again and again? Always rely on our gut instinct when you think something is going on.

Another choice is to stay because of the family. Not everyone is capable to do this. It requires someone who is dedicated to herself, her children and wants the best for the family as a whole unit. They need the father as much as the mother. He is an integral part of the family unit, even when there is turmoil. To stay is partially self-sacrifice since there will be a mental warfare at any given moment on the hurt wanting to come back.

There is an old saying that goes, "Once a cheater, always a cheater!"

According to the American Psychological Association (APA), infidelity in the United states accounted for 20 to 40 percent of divorces.

- According to a study published by the National Institutes of Health (NIH), one partner, in 88 percent of couples studied, cited infidelity as a major contributing factor.
- The vast majority of couples from the NIH study, who divorced, only had one partner who shared infidelity as a major issue.
- People who are under thirty and over seventy were the least likely to divorce after an affair compared to those in their fifties and sixties.
- The APA also cited that 42 percent of divorced individuals reported more than one affair.
- In a Gallup poll, researchers noted that more than half of partners say they would leave their spouse and get a divorce if they found out their spouse was having an affair.
- About 31 percent of married partners would stick it out and not divorce a cheating partner.

We must also include the statistics of affairs for unmarried couples. These cheating statistics are much harder to come by than for married couples. Research shows that unmarried people cheat at double the rate of married couples.

- Biological anthropologist Helen Fisher shares that 60 percent of single men admit to trying to woo an individual away from another relationship to be with them.
- About 53 percent of single women admit they've tried to get another person to leave a committed one.
- A 2018 study of unmarried men and women found that 44 percent of people (men and women) engaged in a relationship of infidelity.

Even God had to deal with an adulterous nation.

> *Then I saw that for all the causes for which backsliding Israel had committed adultery, I had put her away and given her a certificate of divorce; yet her treacherous sister Judah did not fear, but went and played the harlot also.* (Jeremiah 3:8)

The Israelites were worshipping other gods at that time, and anything you put before God is adulterous.

Why Infidelity Leads to Divorce

Cheating can leave both partners feeling confused, angry, and grief-stricken within a marriage. Divorce rates tend to be quite high after an affair has taken place, with studies indicating about half ending in divorce with many partners noting a feeling of betrayal. If you or your partner have cheated, take time to think about whether ending the marriage or *trying to preserve it* is the best choice for both of you.

Divorce Separation

History of Divorce, Origins, and Meaning

Divortere is *divorce*.

To understand the full history of divorce, first, the term should be defined. *Divorce* comes from the Latin word *divortium*, which means "separation." It is also equivalent to the word *divort* or *divortere*. *Di-* means "apart," and *vertere* means "to turn to different ways." *Divertere* was also referred the meaning of "divert, turn aside, separate, or leave one's husband." The word was traced in French vocabulary in the later part of the fourteenth century and in the Middle English in the year 1350–1400.

You both put a lot of thought into what you are leaning toward doing or getting a divorce. You need to think about what caused you to get to this point. Are you willing to try to make it work, or was there adultery that is too much to bear? You need to talk it over and decide together if you seriously consider divorce. Face facts. Will you make the final decision and finally be splitting up? It is not an easy decision for either one of you. You need to put finality to the fighting, confusion, and heartaches. Whatever you decide, you know it will not be easy but has to be done. You need to make a choice. Remember, though, that choices have consequences, so weigh all your choices well.

WHY IS IT HARD TO LET GO AFTER A DIVORCE?

You could possibly grieve the loss of your marriage. Four reasons you may enter the grieving process during and after your divorce are:

- *Because you're still in love or can't let go* loving someone you were attached to, who was part of your daily life. Losing a spouse because of divorce is equal to losing a spouse to death.
- *You relied on your spouse.* You counted on your spouse for years. You are losing both the physical and emotional aspects of the relationship you had with your spouse.
- *You feel like a failure.* You took a marriage vow, and you didn't fulfill it. This leaves you with incompletion of a vow you took before God.
- *Lifestyle changes.* You shared everything together—a home, a family—and you had plans together and dreams of the future. Whether there was a stable relationship or not, divorce means giving up the lifestyle you had (or hoped for) with your spouse. This means a dramatic adjusting to changes in your life.

Emotional Stages of Divorce

1. *Denial*—it is hard to believe it's happening to you. You refuse to accept that the relationship is over, and you keep trying to find solutions to the marital problems. Some use denial to keep from facing the reality of their situation and is a powerful coping tool.
2. *Shock*—you feel numbness, panic, and rage. Life being by yourself commonly causes fear. You sometimes ask, how am I going to *survive a divorce*? These feelings and questions seem impossible to shake.
3. Letting go—at this stage, you know that there is life after divorce, and you give way to hope.
4. *Moving on*—you start to let go and find other venues to fulfill your life.

Here are some Bible verses on divorce. There is no judgment here. You must judge yourself. I was a divorced person also!

> *They said, "Moses permitted a man to write certificates of divorce to dismiss her." And Jesus answered and said to them, "Because of the hardness of your heart he wrote you this precept." But from the beginning of creation, God made them male and female. For this reason, a man shall leave his father and mother and be joined to his*

wife, and the two shall become one flesh, so then they are no longer two but one flesh. Therefore, what God has joined-together, let no man separate. (Mark 10:4–9)

It has been said, "Anyone who divorces his wife must give her a certificate of divorce." I say to you that whoever divorces his wife, except for sexual immorality makes her the victim of adultery, and anyone who marries a divorced woman commits adultery. (Matthew 5:31–32)

And a woman who has a husband who does not believe, if he is willing to live with her, let her not divorce him. For the unbelieving husband is sanctified by the wife, and the unbelieving wife is sanctified by the husband; otherwise, your children would be unclean, but now they are holy. But if the unbeliever depart, let him depart; a brother or a sister is not under bondage in such cases. But God has called us to peace. For wife how do you know, O wife, whether you will save your husband? Or how do you know, O husband, whether you will save your wife? But as God has distributed to each one, as the Lord has called each one, so let him walk. And so I ordain in all the churches. (1 Corinthians 7:13–17)

> *A wife is bound by law as long as her husband lives; but if her husband dies, she is at liberty to be married to whom she wishes, only in the Lord.* (1 Corinthians 7:39)

> *Therefore, I desire that the younger widows marry, bear children, manage the house, give no opportunity to the adversary to speak reproachfully.* (1 Timothy 5:14)

> *But I say to the unmarried and widow, it is good for if they remain even as I am.* (1 Corinthians 7:8)

It all begins when the two of you become one. I know some will question the next statements I make, but here goes.

First, when does oneness occur? In the Bible, when it says, "He knew her," it was when they, to use a modern term, hooked up (aka had sex). There are many examples throughout the Bible, but the very first one shows how it starts.

> *Adam* KNEW *Eve his wife, and she conceived and bore Cain.* (Genesis 4:1)

When there is a scripture in the Bible mentioning that a man *knows* a woman, it means that they had sex.

Another good example would be Mary and Joseph because they were betrothed (engaged). At that time, engagement was considered the same as a marriage, but the consummation (first official act of sexual intercourse between two people) does not occur until they wed.

Then Mary and Joseph were visited by angels.

> *Now the birth of Jesus Christ was as follows: After His mother Mary was betrothed to Joseph, before they* CAME TOGETHER, *she was found to be with child of the Holy Spirit. Then Joseph her husband, being a just man, and not wanting to make her a public example, was minded to put her away secretly. But while he thought about these things, behold an Angel of the Lord appeared to him in a dream, saying, "Joseph son of David, do not be afraid to take to you Mary your wife, for that which she has conceived in her is of the Holy Spirit. And she will bring forth a Son, and you shall call His name Jesus, for He will save His people from their sins. So all this was done that it might be fulfilled which was spoken by the Lord through the prophet, saying, 'Behold, the virgin shall be with child, and bear a Son, and they shall call His name Immanuel, which is translated, 'God with us." Then Joseph, being aroused from sleep, did as the angel of the Lord commanded him and took to him his wife, and did not* KNOW *her till she had brought forth*

> *her firstborn Son. And he called His name Jesus.* (Matthew 1:18–25)

Jesus was in Mary's womb, and this pregnancy had to be sinless. They had to do what the angel said so that the whole birth of Jesus was sin-free. This way, He was without sin and could take our sin on Himself to the cross.

Look at it this way—oneness between a woman and man begins when they had sex the first time. Thus, if you are married and are having sex outside your marriage, you have become one with whomever you have sex with. At this point, the oneness with your marriage partner is broken.

Today, it's common to live together as a trial (the Bible calls that fornication). You have made the commitment, whether you want to admit it or not, with that person you chose, yet you are afraid to make it permanent by marriage.

When death, adultery, or divorce happens, that oneness is broken because the person who made you whole is gone, no matter by which one of the three. Having a death certificate, a divorce paper, or finding out about the adultery is not necessary to confirm it. You know and feel it in your heart! Have you ever watched the program *Cheaters*? They knew in their heart that their partner was being unfaithful before they wanted their partner checked out.

Suddenly you enter uncharted territory—looking for direction with no one there to help you.

> *I will lift up my eyes to the hills—
> from whence comes my help? My help comes*

> *from the Lord who made heaven and earth.*
> (Psalms 121:1–2)

Now is the time to think of planning what you want to do with your life. *Alone!* There, I said it! You need to depend on all that is within you and what you feel you are capable of because now, this is *your* life! You have the control to where you go from here! The time has come to make some choices. You relied on your spouse to help you make decisions, but now, that is missing. In the beginning, it seems scary, but you can do whatever you imagine with God at your side to help you make decisions.

Because you are a woman, you have lost your head covering at this time. Throughout the Bible, a woman always has a male over her—if not her father, then her husband. He was your covering.

> *But I want you to know that the head of every man is Christ, and the head of the woman is man, and the head of Christ is God.* (1 Corinthians 11:3)

> *For this reason the woman ought to have a symbol of authority on her head, because of the angels.* (1 Corinthians 11:10)

The division can be for many reasons besides infidelity. Sometimes, you are just not compatible with each other. You may have been romantically drawn to each other in the beginning but, after time, found out that this was not the whole makeup of either one of you.

There may be many times you differ in the way you think or feel about a lot of things, which you failed to realize at the time you got married. Take the last election of 2020 for instance. This has divided so many people in our country. Sometimes, the division can be so strong that you are unable to deal with it. I used politics as an example; however, it can be social, mental, or physical.

Not all divorces are traumatic since there can be a meeting of the minds, so when you both realize you were not meant for each other, therefore, divorce.

After the divorce is final, at first, it's hard to find where you fit in. You now have a new identity! When you wed, your title was "married." You no longer have that identity but have a new identity! *Divorced!* Some will accept what has happened, and some will judge you and your motives. You need to be settled with yourself so that whatever anyone else thinks of you, you will be able to understand where they are coming from and be okay with their friendship.

Even though you have mixed feelings about being relieved or apprehensive about where to go from here after the finality of divorce, it gives you somewhat of an inner peace because of no more constant conflicts. As for you, you are starting with a clean slate. You are able to move forward if you don't let this separation interfere with how you feel about yourself and how you feel about your confidence and abilities. You can do all the things you wanted to do but was not an aspiration because you were married. However, if you have children, you could be held back on some of the things because of time with the children or financial changes. Otherwise, your life is yours to go as far as your confidence let you!

You now have a "new normal," no matter which of the three separation traumas you experienced.

Now the Statistics—

These numbers were taken from the 2020 US census.

- *Widowed*—male, 3.48 million; female, 11.27 million; total, *14.75 million* in the United States.
- *Divorced*—male, 10.67 million; female, 14.68 million; total, *25.25 million* in the United States.

To comprehend how many people are in the position of divorce by no choice of their own is difficult.

Widows/Divorces added together is *40 million!* Adding the number of adulteries, this would skyrocket! The number of adulteries will never be known because these occurrences are usually done in secret.

Also, the number of people who live together for years, had children together, and split—this number will never be known, and it would be impossible to estimate these occurrences.

These numbers are staggering, especially when you think of all the people that need some understanding, insight, and guidance.

Chapter 3

Who Is This About?

This is about *you*. If you fit in any of the criteria explained in the last two chapters, no matter what changes happen to us at different times in our life, we all have a beginning. Ours just happens to be the loss of oneness with our partner.

I am not claiming to be an expert in these matters. In fact, I am very humble to be able to share what I learned. I went through the stages you did. I am depending on God as I write this. Many times, I have things written down and must change them. I am continually praying over this because I know it is from Him! Also, I want to stay open to His leading.

While writing this, He kept me going as I relied heavily upon Him for His enlightenment and direction. I was apprehensive and uncertain at first, but I trusted God.

*Trust in the Lord with all your heart
and lean not on your own understanding;*

in all your ways acknowledge Him, and He shall direct your paths. (Proverbs 3:5–6)

I loved writing when I was in high school, but little did I know that God was preparing me for what He had in store for me in the future. I never really had to use any writing skills, until I had my business and had to do training meetings and monthly newsletters for my central branch and bi-monthly for my national sales team. I used spiritual principles to prepare the trainings for my team. I would find a topic and asked God to help me incorporate His principles for my training points. God blessed me because I incorporated His Word in my business. My team consisted of one hundred eighty team members and nine managers. If you stay true to Him and His Word, He will bless what you put your hand to.

Because my business required me to do writing, it helped prepare me for this assignment. As I compile this, I am beginning to understand how Noah felt when God asked him to build the ark—a super huge assignment from God. I know—compared to Noah, my task seems small, but I feel as if it is a very massive project.

Writing for my business was something I loved more than other skills I needed for management. However, I never had to do anything of this magnitude before.

This is about you! Where do you stand right now with having been affected by one of the separations? How do you feel about the spot you are in?

The emptiness you feel is real and needs to be filled. Only you can do it.

With God you can have the fulfilling feeling you are needing at the moment. You need to be comfortable in your own skin. Be the person you always wanted to be. Your relationship with God will get you there.

> *But he who is joined to the Lord is one spirit with Him.* (1 Corinthians 6:17)

This is a spiritual oneness with God.

Read the book "Song of Solomon" in the Bible. It has only eight chapters, and the most beautiful love story to ever read—described as the perfect love relationship. Others say that for the Jews, it is the relationship of Israel to God, or for Christians, it is the relationship of Christ to the church. All three are right. It depends on what your eyes are looking at it to be. This is our love story with our spouse. This is God's love story to us. He calls us His beloved.

At this time, can we call Him our Beloved?

Love, to be complete, must include two people. God loves you. Do you love Him?

> *We love Him because He first loved us.* (1 John 4:19)

Looking at the first version, love relationship as being an example for the sake of what I am writing about, look at "Song of Solomon" and how the characters described each other. They are totally focused on each other. They find no fault or flaw! This is how you should perceive your partner until death!

"Song of Solomon" is my SOS because it showed me how to have a healthy love relationship in the home if you don't let "little foxes that spoil the vine," like resentment, arguing, or neglect into your relationships.

In the book of "Song of Solomon," the "little foxes that spoil the vine" can be anything harmful to the relationship—mostly, jumping ahead and fulfilling the desires that you have for each other before the wedding ceremony!

Because of where we are as a society today, couples have lost the Song of Solomon kind of love relationship with each other. Both men and women are guilty of this. They are not holding their spouse up as the best thing that has happened to them, ever! You need to feed this in your marriage constantly to keep that Song of Solomon love relationship alive. With your eyes full of your spouse, you are not looking to see if the grass is greener on the other side. All couples' lives are the same. It is what you do to make your marriage work and be better every day.

Everything in life has a chain of command, whether it is the military, the government, businesses, or life. This happens to be the chain of command for women. In this chain of command, a woman always needs a man to watch over her.

> *But I realize that the head of every man is Christ, and the head of the woman is man, and the head of Christ is God.* (1 Corinthians 11:3)

We then, as widows, victims of adultery, or divorced, need to have a male who would be our head covering because this structure has changed. Without a head covering, you do not have a man who is in charge of watching out for your welfare. You need to get it back ASAP!

How do you do it? By finding a Christ-centered church to attend regularly so you have the church elders to watch out for you in place of your head covering.

> *The* LORD *watches over the strangers:*
> *He relieves the fatherless and widow; but the*
> *way of the wicked He turns upside down.*
> (Psalm 146:9)

When I was divorced, I was going to a more secular church at that time because I was teaching Sunday school and led many youths to the Lord. I immediately went to a local Christ-centered church. There, I felt the protection I needed to make sure I was walking the way the Lord wanted me to.

When you become a widow, victim of adultery, or divorced, you lose your head covering. If you have a son, the oldest son becomes your earthly head covering, in God's eyes. If you do not have a son or a close male relative, to be your head covering, you need to join a Christ-centered church so you can have your head covering back. You would be taking a big, positive step and will feel more confident and secure again to move on. This is your protection from going astray. While your spouse was here, you felt secure and confident. This also is gone. This is our way to get our protection back—by having things in order in our life again. You now have divine protection with the guidance of your church family.

Time has a way of continuing no matter what happens.

> *Days go by on the feet of a turtle; years go by on the wings of a dove.*

Sometimes, this is in your favor, but mostly, you are left to wonder how time can go on since nothing is the same in your life anymore. You wonder how it can continue since your whole world has been turned upside down and basically collapsed. But it does!

I made it a habit to memorize scripture, and these two scriptures really helped me because of the many times I went through the trauma stage.

> *He gave me beauty for ashes, the oil of joy for mourning, the garment of praise for the spirit of heaviness, that they might be trees of righteousness, the planting of the Lord, that He might be glorified.* (Isaiah 61:3 KJV)

> *Thou hast turned my mourning into dancing for me: thou hast put off my sackcloth. Thou hast turned my mourning into dancing for me and girded me with gladness; to the end my glory I sing praise unto thee and not be silent. O Lord my God, I*

> *will give thanks unto thee forever.* (Psalm 30:11–12 KJV)

These are also songs that I sing to help me in times that I need them. It would be a good thing to memorize them and look at them as your helpers.

Singing always lifts your spirit up. You're unable to have stinking thinking when you are trying to remember the words of a song. The best scripture/song for "stinking thinking" is in Philippians.

> *Finally, brethren, whatsoever things are true, whatsoever things are honest, whatsoever things are just, whatsoever things are pure, whatsoever things are lovely, whatsoever things are of good report; if there be any virtue, if there be any praise think on these things.* (Philippians 4:8)

I have six pages of songs that are from the Scripture, and I sing whatever song I need for that day.

Memorizing scripture helps you on those days that you feel your spirit is down. This is when you put your mind on things above and not on what is happening at that time.

> *You will keep him in perfect peace, whose mind is stayed on You. Because he trusts in You.* (Isaiah 26:3)

Only you can change your situation by your response to it.

At this point, what can God do to help you?

I think, now would be a good time to ask God to mold you! What I am referring to is becoming the clay and letting God be the potter!

> *But now, O Lord, You are our Father; we are the clay, and You our potter; And all we are the work of your hand.* (Isaiah 64:8)

> *But indeed, O man, who are you to reply against God? Will the thing formed say to him who formed it, "Why have you made me like this?" Does not the potter have power over the clay, from the same lump to make one vessel for honor and another for dishonor?* (Romans 9:20–21)

This is a big step to take. If you do take it, be prepared to see God working in your life.

Now, you can observe what a great God we serve!

Before you know it, you are counting the years since your spouse has been gone.

Chapter 4

How Does God Feel About Us?

First, we need to see how God sees women, then on to widows. I am taking this approach because there isn't much said in Scripture about women who are divorced or victims of adultery.

Starting with the Old Testament scriptures is best because that is where we find how God set everything up. Then go to the New Testament scriptures to see how Jesus dealt with women. We need to look at both to see how life has evolved for us, not because of God but because of how man has perverted what God thought of us.

As usual, we'll start at the beginning, just like we did in the other chapters.

> *Then God said, "Let Us make man in Our image, according to Our likeness; let them have dominion over the fish of the sea,*

> over the birds of the air, and over the cattle, over all the earth and over every creeping thing that creeps on the earth." So God created man in His own image; in the image of God He created him, male and female He created them. (Genesis 1:26–27)

When you look at the creation of both male and female, you see that they were both created in the image of God. This means we have all the same rights of man, except that man is always the head because he was made ahead of the woman. We were created in God's image. Just what is the image of God?

First, God said, "Let *us* make man in our image." The *us* is the trinity, the threefold being of God—God the Father, God the Son (Jesus), and God the Holy Spirit. The image of God is triune. Being triune is how we were created in God's image—body, soul, and spirit. The answer is in the Scripture.

> Now may the God of peace Himself sanctify you completely; and may your whole spirit, soul, and body be preserved blameless at the coming of our Lord Jesus Christ. (1 Thessalonians 5:23)

Man and woman contain the same makeup from God. The body, because of reproduction, is the only difference. The soul is the seat of the senses, desires, affections, and appetites, while the spirit is the part of us that *connects or refuses to connect to God.*

> *And Adam said, "This is now bone of my bones, and flesh of my flesh: She shall be called Woman because she was taken out of Man."* (Genesis 2:23)

Can't you see the love expressed in how Adam looked at Eve? Can't you see how he felt about the woman there beside him? Even in naming Eve Woman, God had a part in man's naming of the woman. This shows us how much Adam cared for himself. When I say cared for himself, I mean you take care that you refrain from hurting yourself or take physical risks to hurt yourself. Any man who is unable to love himself, not egotistical, is incapable of ever really loving a woman.

Imagine—Adam was alone with God. What a wonderful place to be. He had total access to God anytime he wanted it. (We do, too, because God is omnipresent.) And then, God took a part of Adam and created another being! You better believe Adam was extremely glad to have someone there with him at his side. Doing things together is always better, even to share God.

It was never written in Scripture how long Adam was alone. The timing could make a difference in his loving care of Eve. Loneliness makes the heart grow fonder.

This was good while it lasted for both man and woman. Then came the disobedience against what God told him about not touching the fruit. This disobedience was what opened the door to sin for all humanity.

> *And out of the ground the Lord God made every tree grow that is pleasant to the sight and good for food. The tree of life was also, in the midst of the garden, and the tree of the knowledge of good and evil.*
>
> *Then the Lord God took the man and put him in the garden of Eden to tend and keep it. And the Lord God commanded the man saying, "Of every tree of the garden you may freely eat; but of the tree of the knowledge of good and evil you shall not eat, for in the day you eat of it you shall surely die."* (Genesis 2:9, 15–17)

> *Now the serpent [Satan] was more cunning than any beast of the field which the Lord has made. And the serpent said to the woman, "Has not God indeed said, "You shall not eat of every tree of the garden?"" And the woman said to the serpent, "We may eat of the fruit of the trees of the garden; but the tree which is in the midst of the garden, God said, 'You shall not eat it, nor shall you touch it, lest you die.'" Then the serpent said to the woman, "You will not surely die." For God knows that in the day you eat of it your eyes will be opened and you will be like*

> *God, knowing good and evil. So, the woman saw that the tree was good for food that it was pleasant to the eyes, and a tree desirable to make one wise, so she took of its fruit and ate. She also gave to her husband with her and he ate. Then the eyes of both of them were opened, and they knew that they were naked: and they sewed fig leaves together and made themselves coverings.* (Genesis 3:1–7)

God told Adam about not touching the fruit. But then, Eve ate of the fruit and told Adam to eat of the fruit also! Eve did it with her head covering, Adam was present with his participation, and he made no attempt to stop her or question her actions. Adam failed Eve because he was her head covering and did not stop her. Because of this disobedience, they opened sin up to all humanity. (Romans 5)

It did not take very much time for things to change drastically for the woman. Not sure when it started or how things changed but I think of the frog in a pan of water, and when you turn up the heat slowly, the frog does not notice the change until it's too late. This was probably what happened over time, with the changes of how women were treated.

As time went on, women were looked at differently. In fact, it came to the point that they were looked at as being beneath the slave. Wow! What a change.

Why does the Bible say so much about widows? It is all over the scriptures. It is mentioned fifty-five times in the

Old Testament and twenty-six times in the New Testament. As you can see, God has a lot to say about widows. Why?

Fundamentally, God knows and holds dear the weak and helpless. Widows and orphans have a special place in God's eyes!

In the Bible God has a lot to say about widows. If you read the prophets, the psalms, the gospels, and the letters to the churches in the New Testament, you are unable to read far without the subject of widows coming up.

When the nation Israel turned away from God, they also turned away from His commandments. The ones who suffered when this happened were the widows. They were one of the first casualties. Those who wronged widows were reproached by the Old Testament prophets and called Israel back to their God-given responsibilities.

> *In you they have made light of father and mother; in your midst they have oppressed the stranger; in you they have mistreated the fatherless and the widow.* (Ezekiel 22:7)

> *Father of the fatherless and protector of the widows is God in His holy habitation.* (Psalm 68:5)

> *He administers justice for the fatherless and the widow, and loves the stranger, giving him food and clothing.* (Deuteronomy 10:18)

> *If I have withheld anything that the poor desired or have caused the eyes of the widow to fail.* (Job 31:16 NAS)
>
> *The Lord tears down the house of the proud but maintains the widow's boundaries.* (Proverbs 15:25)
>
> *Leave your fatherless children; I will preserve them alive; and let your widows trust in me.* (Jeremiah 49:11)
>
> *You shall not mistreat any widow or fatherless child. If you do mistreat them and they cry out to me, I will surely hear their cry and my wrath will burn and I will kill you with the sword, and your wives shall become Widows and your children fatherless.* (Exodus 22:23–24 ESV)

I picked the five verses above, out of fifteen pages about widows. There are many more. You see how much God cared that the widow was taken care of and protected. Even Job knew where the widows stood because he wanted to make sure that he did not withhold anything from the widow so they didn't cry out to God. He knew God—that if they would cry out to God, He would surely hear widows, and God would burn with wrath. God gave instructions on how to deal with widows in the Old Testament. Nothing escapes God's notice, and He will avenge the orphans and widows.

How were women viewed in ancient Israel before Jesus came? The Jews had a dim view of the Jewish woman. They were treated like how the Middle East women are still treated today. Women were largely uneducated because they were not allowed to receive an education. The only training women had was how to raise the children and keep the home. A woman had no choice in her marriage—her father decided that for her. Under no condition was a woman allowed to divorce her husband. Only a man could initiate a divorce. Why? Because we were made to be helpers. We women always knew men could not manage without us women! This is a good thing. It is more clearly explained in:

> *And the Lord said, "It is not good that man should be alone; I will make him a helper comparable to him."* (Genesis 2:18)

> *Now the Lord God said, "It is not good* [beneficial] *for the man to be alone; I will make him a helper* [one who balances him—a counterpart who is] *suitable and complimentary for him.* (Genesis 2:18 AMP)

In the beginning, God created woman as a helper for man. I put the same scripture from two translations to help you to understand your importance as a woman.

There was only one other time that *helper* as a noun was used, and that was about the Holy Spirit being your spiritual Helper.

> *And I will pray the Father, and the He will give you another Helper that He may abide with you forever.* (John 14:16)

> *But the Helper, the Holy Spirit, whom the Father will send in My name, He will teach you all things, and bring to your remembrance all things that I said to you.* (John 14:26)

The woman was made to be a helper for the physical needs of man. The Holy Spirit came to be a Helper to man's spiritual needs. This is the main reasons why widows and victims of adultery or divorce feel so lost. Their job as a helper to man has ended when their significant other was gone, both physically, mentally, and spiritually.

Women, in New Testament time, were considered extremely low on the scale of standings in humanity. Men refrained talking to them in public because he would have been looked at poorly.

In the New Testament, Jesus, God in the flesh, regularly approached and talked to women. The women were also present when Jesus talked to the people where there were multitudes in the crowds.

How did Jesus and the churches deal with women and widows in the New Testament? Jesus's examples will give God's view, not man's view.

Check out the books of the Bible—Matthew, Mark, Luke, and John—to see the many references to Jesus's interaction with women. He was focused on setting new standards of life and on being about His Father's business. In those four books, Jesus used parables forty-five times and only once in the book of John, for a total of forty-six times. What is a parable? A parable is a story that has another meaning.

Jesus gives us many parables in the Bible. Why does He use parables—to hide or clarify the meaning?

The word *parable* is from the root word *paraballo* or *parabole* in Greek. This compound word comes from *para*, which means "to come alongside or compare," and *ballo*, which literally means "to throw" or "see" with.

Even though there are a lot of lessons to be learned from all the parables, the only two parables that I will use has to do with women and widows. They are in the book of Luke.

> *So he spoke this parable to them saying: "What man of you, having a hundred sheep, if he loses one of them, does not leave the ninety-nine in the wilderness, and go after one which is lost until he finds it? And when he has found it, he lays it on his shoulders, rejoicing. And when he comes home, he calls together his friends and neighbors, saying*

to them, 'Rejoice with me, for I have found my sheep which was lost!' I say to you that likewise there will be more joy in heaven over one sinner who repents than over ninety-nine just persons who need no repentance. Or what WOMAN *having ten silver coin, if she loses one coin, does not light a lamp sweep the house, and search carefully until she finds it? And when she has found it, she calls her friends and neighbors together, saying, 'Rejoice with me, for I have found the piece which I lost!' Likewise, I say to you, there is joy in the presence of the angels of God over one sinner who repents."* (Luke 15:3–10)

Then He spoke a parable to them, that men always ought to pray and not lose heart, saying: "There was in a certain city a judge who did not fear god nor regard man. Now there was a widow in that city; and she came to him, saying, 'Get justice from my adversary.' And he would not for a while, but afterward he said within himself, "Though I do not fear God nor regard man, yet because this widow troubles me I will avenge her lest by her continual coming she weary me."' Then the Lord said, "Hear what the unjust judge said, and shall not God not avenge His own elect who cry out

> *day and night to Him, though He bears long with them? I tell you that He will avenge them speedily. Nevertheless, when the Son of Man comes, will He really find faith on the earth?"* (Luke 18:1–8)

You need to keep on praying and asking.

> *Yet you do not have because you do not ask. You ask and do not receive, because you ask amiss, that you may spend it on your pleasure.* (James 4:2–3)

Many times we tend not to ask for what we need or want. Today women who are in our spot as widows, victims of adultery, and divorced are looked at as inferior in some circumstances. Our standing is considered "lower" in the normal family structure, and rightfully so, this is because of no fault of our own. we show partiality to those who have a better social standing, whether your status is with money, worldly goods, marital, or how high you rose in society. No one is exempt from this, we are all very judgmental.

> *He will surely rebuke you if you secretly show partiality.* (Job 13:10 KJV)

> *Yet He is not partial to princes, nor does He regard the rich more than the poor; for they are all the work of His hands.* (Job 34:19)

Jesus being perfect and is not a respecter of persons, everyone is the same in His eyes. He looks at everyone equally. He looks at every man/woman equally. Matthew has the best example of this.

> *While still talking to the multitudes, behold, His mother and brothers stood outside seeking to speak with Him. Then one said to Him, "Look, your mother and your brothers are standing outside, seeking to speak with you." But He answered and said to the one who told Him, "Who is My mother and who are My brothers?" And He stretched out His hand toward His disciples and said, "Here are my mother and My brothers: For whoever does the will of My father in heaven is My brother and sister and mother."* (Matthew 12:46–50)

Which makes us ask this question: "What would Jesus do?" WWJD was popular in the 1990s. At that time, it was not a recent move but has been around over one hundred years. Charles M. Sheldon, minister and evangelist Christian writer, used it in his 1807 novel *In His Steps: What Would Jesus Do?* Trying to be like Jesus has been around for a long time. Sheldon was a national leader in what was referred to as the Social Gospel movement. He put social issues at the forefront of religious life. This brings to mind that at all times, especially moral decisions, always look at Jesus's life and reflect on how he handled it.

Since Joseph, Jesus's father, had passed on, the eldest son was considered the woman's head covering. Jesus, being the oldest son, was considered His mother's head covering and was well aware of that fact. He showed how important it was when He was on the cross. He knew the structure that God set up for women.

At the cross, Jesus literally gave His mother to John the disciple. He made sure she had an earthly head covering.

> *Now then stood by the cross of Jesus His mother, and His mother's sister, Mary the wife of Clopas, and Mary Magdalene. When Jesus therefore saw His mother, and the disciples whom He loved standing by, He said to His mother, "Woman, behold your son!" Then He said to the disciple, "Behold your mother!" And from that hour that disciple took her to his own home.* (John 19:25–27)

The woman caught in adultery is a good example of how Jesus interacted *with a woman who lived in a questionable lifestyle. This story is in the book of John.*

> *Then the scribes and Pharisees brought to Him a woman caught in adultery. And when they had set her in the midst, they said to Him, "Teacher, this woman was caught in adultery, in the very act. Now Moses, in the law, commanded us that such should be stoned. But what do You say?" This they said,*

> *testing Him, that they might have something of which to accuse Him. But Jesus stooped down and wrote on the ground with His finger, as though He did not hear. When they continued asking Him, He raised Himself up and said to them, "He who is without sin among you, let him throw a stone at her first." And again, He stooped down and wrote on the ground. Then those who heard it, being convicted by their conscience, went out one by one, beginning with the oldest even to the last. And Jesus was left alone, and the woman standing in the midst. When Jesus had raised Himself up and saw no one, but the woman. He said to her, "Woman where are those accusers of yours? Has no one condemned you?" She said, "No one, Lord." And Jesus said to her, "Neither do I condemn you; go and sin no more."* (John 8:3–11)

We need to confess our sins and ask for forgiveness of the wrong things we have done. We are all sinners in need of having Jesus, who died on the cross for us so that it was possible to clean up our act.

What Jesus said, I'll say to you, "Go and sin no more."

One of the first and necessary steps on your road to moving ahead is self-examination about your shortcomings, faults, and sins. Deep down, we know when we are doing wrong but never want to admit it. You need to depend on your God-given gut instinct to let you know when we are doing wrong. You know what's being said is true because you've all experienced it at one time or another. This is the Holy Spirit helping you feel uncomfortable in those situations.

We all have faults, and we all become set in our ways to some degree. You need to be ready for change and forget the way you always did things to change and move on to the next level God has in store for you. Be the clay! I know you can do it because there were numerous times when I had to change what I was doing, and you know what? I lived!

Start getting ready for the new you that is about to surprise you—that you could or would even do some of the things God will be leading you into.

As you start on the new journey, I'm excited for what lies ahead for you. You will also see that life is becoming exciting each day as you see God work in your life. There is a saying, "You get what you expect." Set your expectations high so no matter where you end up, you'll be excited—because it is way above what you thought was your fate as a widow, victim of adultery, or divorced would have ever been.

Always remember to daily remind God of your talents and that you are waiting for the assignment He has in store for you.

Start looking forward to your new life and all the assignments that God has for you to do. At first, this is hard to see, but whatever your heart starts leading you to that will help someone else, this is where you start. As you start, God will reveal to you what you need to do with what He put on your heart. He lives there, so He knows better than even you do which way you are drawn to go. Listen to the Holy Spirit. Pray, trust, and obey Him.

Noah is a prime example of this. He knew how to listen to God. His whole lifestyle changed when God told him to build an ark and gave Noah instructions for the task.

The first step is to "listen." This is the step most of us fail because we are busy talking or asking when we pray.

The second step is to "trust." Noah trusted God and what He asked him to do.

The third step is to "obey." Noah obeyed God's instructions to the letter. Noah was chosen for this purpose because of who he was, not because of his standing in society but what God saw in him. God's reason for choosing Noah are shown in Genesis.

> *But Noah found grace in the eyes of God. Noah was a just man, perfect in his generations. Noah walked with God.* (Genesis 6:8, 9)

The song "Trust and Obey" is one of my favorites, but I sing "listen," trust, and obey!

Trust and Obey.
Listen, Trust and Obey.
There's no other way,
To be happy with Jesus,
Than to *listen*, trust and obey.

Chapter 5

WHAT MADE US WHO WE ARE?

There is a story behind each one of us and where we are today. No matter what changes happen to us at different times in our life, we all have a beginning that makes us who we are. The different traumas in our lives made us a different person than when we were before each trauma happened—any of these traumas will be detrimental to how we as a widow, victim of adultery, or divorced deal with spousal separation trauma.

Why did I show you how God started our paths, like the example of Adam and Eve in Genesis 4:1? Why should we look back?

We learn from our past and from the great people who gave us examples to follow.

You are unable to move forward without looking back. You need to look at what you did right, and you need to also ask for forgiveness for your mistakes (sins).

Because of my history and what I went through, I can see how I could do a lot of the things that most women were unable to do. I am sharing my story to show you how things worked in my life. However, you should think of things about yourself so that you can see how your own story made you who you are. I want you to take notes of things about you. Note where you had joyous happenings because without joys, there would be no traumas in your life and how you dealt with them both. This includes all joys and trauma. There are many traumas you had earlier in your life and forgot about. Going back is hard because some are buried so deep that you always tried not to remember them. Ask God to help you so you have a full picture of who you are. You need to list them here, but be sure to highlight any of the marital joys and trauma since this is what we are focusing on. It will be of the utmost help for you to see how you went through other traumas because they define who you are.

I am unable to say I understand your history because this is your life, and only you know what your experiences were and how they affected you. Everyone has a different experience, but there are always some similarities in things that happened that were right and in things we did that were wrong.

In fact, I want you to stop reading and get a tablet or notebook to write your story. Why? This will help you to look back and see how far you've come. Use this later so you can see how you progressed through the different traumas you had. What happened in your life? Where did you see God's hand in getting you to where you are at today? You could skip this, but you will miss out on evaluating yourself and miss understanding what made you who you are today.

Start reading again when you have completed this so you can get a better understanding of yourself.

Who are your friends? This way, you see what part they played to help your progress. Make a list. How did they help you? What are your interests and hobbies? Make a list. What part did they play to define your life? How did they shape you? What part did they play to make you who you are? What plans do you have to help you move forward from today? What haven't you done yet that you always wanted to do? Think big! Chart a strategy. List what steps are necessary to reach your plan. What are your plans to move forward? When you make plans, think bigger than you ever did before. Look for something you can get involved in or that you do well. God gave us all talents. Ask God what is your assignment. He wants to use you in some way.

We all have a starting point. The only reason I'm sharing mine is because it took many years to get to where I am now. This will help you to understand why God put the assignment on my heart to share this with you.

Please do not judge or pity me. All I ask is understanding because it is my life and the choices I made. The decisions I made were because of a deep love for God, my husband, and my children. This is what was best for me at the time. I am a private person, and I never liked sharing personal things because I liked staying in the background, but I feel that the information is necessary for you to understand that I have been at some low places. Everyone's story is unique to themselves and yet have similarities. The different twists along the way are what make you, you.

Although I want you to be sure to list all the traumas, list the joys along the way also. There is always a joy before a trauma. All joys do not end up as traumas.

My first traumatic experience was when I was a toddler. I loved my dad very much, and during the daytime, he was a wonderful dad (the joy before the trauma). My father was an alcoholic and not a good one. He changed when he was drunk and was nasty at this time. It usually happened at night when he came home intoxicated, and he would look for us (I had two older brothers), and of course we would be in bed sleeping. This was when the beatings happened. We learned quickly that when we heard him come home drunk at night, we would hide under our beds because he was too drunk to get to us there, and this was our way of not getting a beating. (You could say that the taste for alcohol was beaten out of me at an early age!) It is amazing how God put a way of escape in our hearts at such an early stage. I am unaware at what point these beatings stopped but was extremely glad they did. Joy! I learned acceptance and forgiveness of being hurt at an early age even if I didn't know the proper way to do it. My dad and I had an extremely special bond. When I was five years old, he taught me how to shoot a .22 rifle. We would go target shooting regularly. My brothers weren't interest in target shooting, but I loved it and still do today! This gave me more time with my dad. Joys are stronger than trauma and become lasting memory.

I had a pretty normal, uneventful rest of my youth—nothing extreme in the joys or traumas.

My mother went to Sunday school every week when she was growing up. She had nine pins for perfect attendance. In all my years, I never remembered her reading the Bible or ever mentioning God to me once. I remember going to Sunday school one time when I was in second grade and I loved it. This was my first remembrance of an encounter with God. Big joy! However, when I turned fifteen, she wanted me to get confirmed. At this time, I wasn't even baptized yet. Therefore, I had to be baptized before I could get confirmed. This was my first real introduction to God and His Word. I loved the memorization of scriptures and learning about Him. I was touched deeply in my heart but was unaware of what this all meant at that time. This was the beginning of my heart being open to God, church, and His Word.

Before I explain this next event, I must explain about my mother. She was my hero! She had to quit school when she was in sixth grade. Her mother (my grandmother) broke her leg, and there were seven siblings that needed to be taken care of. My mother was the oldest daughter. She was taking care of her brothers and sister, and there was a sister that was two years old, plus her mother with the broken leg. She was doing the chores for everyone and, mind you, at the age of twelve. They didn't have running water, so this wasn't an easy task! I just want you to understand where my mother's mindset came from. A woman's place was to have a family because she thought this was the only choice for women. This will help you to understand what happens next.

My older brothers didn't work while they were in high school. This is only being used as a reference to show you the different way girls were thought of at that time.

When I turned sixteen, my mother said I had to quit school and go to work to pay board. It wasn't that I loved school, but I loved learning. This was to me my saving grace to go further than any other way possible, and my grades reflected my commitment. I had to do some very deep thinking to finish school. Because I lacked parental support to finish high school, I knew that there weren't any chances for me to have a shot at higher learning. I knew I would probably end up with what my mother's fate was, but I wanted more. I wanted to be able to help my children by supporting them in whatever they wanted to do and break the stigma that a woman's place is just in the home but that they could do and be more.

It was a huge commitment to make for the next two years until I graduated. I'm not sure if you can call this a trauma, but this joy came after the trauma! However, it did change my life for the next two years, and I guess you could say forever. Because my mother wanted me to quit school and get a job to pay board, I would not be defiant or disrespectful of what my mother wanted me to do. I compromised and asked her if I could stay in school if I got a job after school to pay the $20 per week she wanted. She agreed, and I was very thankful that we worked out a solution so I could finish high school. It was a big commitment, but to be able to graduate was what I wanted more than anything in the world. I knew I needed a high school degree if I wanted to make anything of myself.

I applied for a job at Paris Neckware, Walnutport, Pennsylvania, and I got the job as a sewer of handkerchiefs for a dollar an hour. One good thing was that I worked for piecework, so my wagers were higher. I was so excited that my plan was working out.

Now, to the initiation of the plan. I would always wear skirts to school, so after I walked eight-tenth of a mile home from school. (The walkers are still doing this today. I am just showing this for the schedule I kept in order to graduate.) I would stop at home, which was on the way to my job, and change the skirt to jeans, walked three-tenth of a mile to my job, and worked from three in the afternoon until nine at night. I would then walk three-tenth of a mile back home and do my homework for the next school day. I never attended any sporting events that the school had at any time because my education was more important than any sporting event could ever be. I always worked every Saturday that I was able to so I could increase my paycheck. I was responsible for anything I needed for myself or for school from this point forward. So just like my mother, I was responsible for myself at an early age. My pay for the week averaged $37.50 and twenty went to my mother, so I had $17.50 for myself for the week. I was very frugal and watched every cent that went out of my pocket.

I am only sharing this to show you how strongly I wanted my diploma and how disciplined I was to achieve it. The extreme joy was that I did graduate and was on the honor roll. It was when I was in eleventh or twelfth grade when I was eleventh rank out of one hundred thirty-one—not bad for the commitment I had the last two years of high school.

The next joy was that I met Clark the man, who would become my husband, around the time I started working. We dated while I worked and knew that we would get married eventually. After a year of dating, we made plans to get married five months after I graduated. We were married at Neffs UCC Church in Neffs, Pennsylvania, and I became a Neff! My husband's great-great-grandfather helped build the Neffs church. This great-great-grandfather was on the mother's side of my husband, so his name wasn't Neff. Our wedding was two and a half years after we met. I had an early joy because when I got married, I was three months pregnant. I was wrong in doing this, and as I look back, I found so many things I needed forgiveness for. Thank you, Jesus, for taking my sins away! I am grateful that he helped me visualize my dream and respected the commitment I made. This was a big joy!

My husband's mother, Katie, who would be my future mother-in-law, was a big influence on me spiritually. She impressed me with her love of the Lord and how she loved reading the Bible.

We were married six months before his mother passed at fifty-four years in June of colon cancer. She held on because she was looking forward to seeing our first baby, Wanda, born in May. Joy, joy, joy! No one seemed to want Katie's most precious thing—her Bible. I took her Bible and started reading it. This was when I was nineteen.

After that, I started to search and research scripture—not just reading. My hunger was not satisfied with just reading any longer. I learned to love God's Word and all that He has there for me. To me, it was like a treasure—to find it, you just need to dig, or it is just like a big puzzle that you could put together if you took the time to search for your answers and, of course, with God's help and guidance. The love of learning that I acquired in school just continued with learning about God.

I had a good *Strong's Exhaustive Concordance* that was given to me by a gentleman who was eighty-six years old. He saw my enthusiasm for the Word of God. It was a big help because there were very few resources available back then—not as many as you have available today with the internet and computers. Oh my God! And we survived! I used to make my own spreadsheets—before Excel—of things I was trying to understand, to have greater insight into the topics that I was studying. This was my recreation time because I was busy raising my family and needed an outlet.

> *For everyone to whom much has been given, from him much will be required; and to whom much has been committed, of him they will ask the more.* (Luke 12:48)

Because of dealing with many huge assignments in my life, God knew I could handle them.

My first big assignment was motherhood. This was the biggest joy of my life. I was the mother of four children—two girls, Wanda and Laura, and twin boys, Keith and

Kevin. They were the ultimate JOY of my life! Laura, the youngest daughter, was only twenty-two months old when the twins were born. As a twenty-five-year-old woman, I had my hands full! At that time, my husband had to take a part-time job, also because of the extra responsibility we had on our plate since I could not go back to work. They did not have day care then, and it was difficult to find a babysitter for three small children. This left me with full responsibility of the household. So I was used to having this responsibility, and now, I was doing it without him—taking care of the bills, any problems that came up each day, car issues, and doctor visits with four. The grocery shopping was a special trip with two babies in my cart and my eldest daughter with my second daughter and the groceries in her cart.

Things were challenging at that time, but with prayer and just doing what we had to do, we moved on no matter what. This is a good lesson to apply to any challenges that come your way. They can be learning experiences that God can use to help you grow. By incorporating fun things in the daily things you do with the children makes it more fun—not knowing at that time how much this was preparing me for future widowhood.

As far as the time with my children, I was glad for the five years I could be at home to enjoy their early years of being there to train them and to study God's Word.

> *Train up a child in the way he should go and when he is old, he will not depart from it.* (Proverbs 22:6)

Because of gaining knowledge, I was able to help them in many ways I would have been unable to if I have had worked for those five years. It was a blessing for me to raise my kids and to be able to be into the Word as much as I was. I thoroughly enjoyed my time with the kids and was thankful for the time God gave me to be with them. As I looked back, my kids were the biggest blessing of my entire life.

My kids and I would memorize scriptures together. I found that scriptures were much easier to memorize by singing songs, especially if there was a *catchy tune*. We especially loved singing this one:

> *Beloved let us love one another for love is of God and everyone that loveth is born of God. He that loveth not knoweth not God for God is love. So beloved let us love one another.* (1 John 4:7–8 KJV)

These are the words of the song found in John 4:7–8 (KJV). The words of songs ending has where it is located in the Bible.

I shared with them how to use the Bible to look up some of the songs we would sing so they knew where the songs came from. We memorized the books of the Bible together. I needed it as much as they did—don't we all? We played a game where I would give them a scripture—they would all wait patiently with their Bibles closed to make it fair. When I say, "Go," they would race to look it up. I kept track of who found it first, and they had to start reading it to show they found it. The one who found it first would be rewarded with some sort of treat. Today, my kids are extremely competitive, independent, confident, and intelligent. I know it is because of all these things in their early childhood. No matter how old they are, they will always be my kids! Doesn't everyone feel that way?

Memorizing the books of the Bible are needed to make it easier to find scriptures. How can you find something if you don't know where to look for it? Why do you have to look at the "Table of Contents" to find the book that the pastor is referring to. We need to take the time to teach them how to use what our whole religion is based on—the Word of God. Sunday School was a must because this was a great foundation for them. They learn great stories that are in the Bible. Also, introducing your children to God, Jesus, and the Holy Spirit is what most people do not take the time to do. This is one of the most important things you can do for your kids, plus spending time with them. How do you spell love? *Time!*

When my twins were three years old, I found out that my husband was having an affair. I knew it before it actually came to light. This was my *first marital trauma*. I confronted both my husband, her, and her husband was present. By putting light on something, the things in secret end. He asked for forgiveness, and I forgave him.

> *The thing I greatly feared has come upon me.* (Job 3:25)

The trauma of this was so overwhelming that when I took a shower, I cried out to God to take me. The hurt, betrayal, and embarrassment were unbearable. I no longer wanted to live with how I felt and wanted to die.

> *Who long for death, but it does not come, and search for it more than hidden treasure.* (Job 3:21)

Thank God that this prayer was unanswered. He knows that when you are in a state of shock, the prayer is dumb.

When the twins were four, I went back to work and started at General Electric, Allentown, Pennsylvania. I only worked five years at General Electric when I found out my husband was having an affair again. My *second marital trauma*. Because of adultery, I asked him to leave, and I got a divorce. At this time, I asked God to be my head covering and husband since I was without my husband. I may have been wrong spiritually and scripturally, but I knew that He said He was our husband. I knew I needed a head covering.

> *For your Maker is your husband, The Lord of hosts is His name; and your Redeemer is the Holy One of Israel. He is called the God of the whole earth.* (Isaiah 54:5)

I did ask God for forgiveness if I was scripturally wrong at that time. I did not know if it was all right to do this.

Since then I researched this and found out it is okay for any unmarried woman to do.

The kids were younger—the oldest was fifteen, next was eleven, and the twins were nine. The night before the divorce was final, my husband asked if I could stop the divorce because he wanted to come back. I said no on stopping the divorce. I refused! But I would forgive him and let him visit the kids more and be friends again. We were separated for three years. I paid him off for the house, giving him half of what it was worth. I kept the house to keep things as normal as possible for the kids. Everything I did was with their stability and welfare in mind. I know I made mistakes along the way, but I have asked for forgiveness. No one is perfect.

> *For all have sinned and fall short of the glory of God.* (Romans 3:23)

It's amazing the things you can do with God at your side and with prayer. All you need to do is put your mind to it and believe in the Word of God! Here are some examples of this—I put brake lining on my car, changed the oil in my car, and dug a hole when the water pump died. I was unable to afford much, raising four on my own! I kept busy taking care of things—painting the windows on the inside of the house in the winter, just looking for things that needed taking care of to keep busy. You need to keep yourself busy because idle hands give Satan that time to come in and entice you to sin. And of course, I continued with church and reading the Bible. Everything was going good for me, and I had a solid job to rely on.

He then asked me to marry him again. This was unexpected! I had to do a lot of serious thinking. Because of my husband's track record, did I want to take a chance—again? When we divorced, I bought him out, and everything was in my name. I knew I stood to lose everything if things didn't work out the second time because he would be entitled to get half of everything—again. I went into this with my eyes fully open. I said, "Yes."

You probably are thinking, *Why would she marry him again? Why would she trust him again?* These questions have haunted me a lot until I read about Hosea. Hosea was a well-respected minister and prophet. He did the same three things Noah did. He listened, trusted, and obeyed God. Here's how; God told him to marry a harlot. Could you imagine if your pastor did that today? It would be the scandal of the year! He trusted God. Gomer, a harlot, became his wife. Gomer and Hosea had three children together. After Gomer had the children, she longed for her old life and went back into harlotry. Then God said to Hosea, "Go again, love a woman who is loved by a lover and is committing adultery." So Hosea bought Gomer for fifteen shekels of silver and one and one-half homers of barley.

This is what real love will do. It has nothing to do with all that is going on around you at the time, but the question really is: Do you have love? Does your love measure up? Are you able to forgive no matter what?

We remarried on the same date as our first marriage, only twenty years later. I saw firsthand how the divorce affected the kids, so I agreed with one condition. Even though we *knew* (had sex with) each other when we were married before, I told him there could be no sex before we remarried. In my mind, I thought that then, I would see how serious he was. I thought that maybe that was why the first marriage failed—because of having sex during our engagement. I wanted to stick with what I saw was right in God's eyes.

When we did remarry, there was no premarriage sexual involvement, and the kids were aware of it. Never underestimate kids. They know what is going on. They decorated the bedroom with toilet paper, to our surprise, when we got home from the wedding ceremony.

I know the remarriage was for the best, for everyone, especially the kids and future grandkids. Grandkids were not on my mind at that time since there weren't any yet. My decision was right because my husband was a big part of the lives of our grandkids too! No regrets in our getting back together because I know the whole family is necessary for the welfare of future generations.

I continued to work at General Electric for a total of fourteen and a half years on the assembly line, along with other numerous jobs, as they moved me because of my low service time. We were remarried before they closed the Allentown General Electric Plant, then I needed something else to fill my time. God didn't waste any time opening a new door for me.

Remarkably, my church was starting a satellite school to become a pastor. It was through Word of Faith, Dallas,

Texas. I registered and took three semesters. I did remarkably well.

Fall courses were wonderful wisdom, freedom from bondage, alien entities and angels, and I got credits for living word 3, life of Jesus 2, to catch a thief 1, the local church 1, blood covenant 1, and spiritual growth 1.

For winter courses, I had Hebrews, John, James, and Ephesians, with credits in how to cope 1, Psalms 3, evangelism 1, God and government 1, laws of prosperity 2, the new creation 1.

For spring courses, I had the Holy Spirit, life and power of Word, rebuilding the wall (Nehemiah), Joel, and I got credits in New Testament concept 3, spirit of excellence 2, life and power of words 1, how to cope 2, laws of faith 1, the American covenant 1, and mastering the human mind 1.

The reason I'm sharing the courses is to show that I have had some formal education and well-rounded training. By the way, I passed with only two Bs—one in angels and the other in Ephesians. The rest were As. My church was unable to continue with the satellite school. I would have to transfer to another place in Bethlehem, Pennsylvania. Because of the extra miles, I was unable to continue with schooling because of losing the extra family time. As much as I love learning, I know sometimes God closes a door for a reason.

We were active in the church. It was the best times we had together as a family.

Then came my business with the Longaberger Company (baskets)—another joy! I went to a show and loved the product and the company. The thought—that's how God talks to you—came to me to become a sales consultant. I had one problem though. I was unable to talk in front of people! I prayed about it, and this was the direction I got from God:

> *Blessed shall be your basket!*
> (Deuteronomy 28:5)

God opened another door and showed me that this was the direction He wanted me to go! He was right because He blessed me to become National Sales Leader—the highest position you can go in the company. My team consisted of one hundred eighty consultants and nine managers, with sales around one and a half million dollars per year. However, my first show stank! I had a lot of *um* and *um* and *ums*! I asked my daughter to critique me, so I nipped it in the bud early.

I worked hard at building my business. This took up a lot of my time, and I was not in the Word as much as I used to be, except mostly to use scriptural principles to help me with training my team. I read a lot of books on how to have a successful business that used scripture principles. This was the reason my team was so successful. I relied on God and His Word. I was more distracted with what was happening in our marriage than what I realized.

The first ten years of our remarriage was great. We were regularly involved in the church. Being in the fellowship of others helps with your relationship.

We all have things in our past that we regret doing, but we have a forgiving God. Jesus went to the cross for your sins. Your sins are already paid for. All you need to do is ask Him for forgiveness of your sins and be specific and for Him to cleanse you from all unrighteousness. Boom! Forgiveness is done! While talking to Him, it would help you to be able to move forward if you opened your heart to Him to come in and make you whole.

My kids were getting older, and I had more time to work on my business. Our involvement with the church tapered off since the kids were either at school or in the Army. It seemed like the family was not as close as we used to be without anything happening that you could point to an extreme event! Other than that, life moved on. We got together for holidays and kept communications going. I loved having us together as a family.

No matter what, you need to keep involved with the church and the functions of the church. It is easier to give in to sin if you don't attend regularly. So, my husband started to avoid church by working on Sundays. Because of not being involved with the church and not having the light shine on his life, he gave in to continually being unfaithful. My many *marital traumas*. Satan knows your weaknesses, and you need to be aware all the time because of this. My husband had a problem but would not admit it, so he did not seek help. You must admit you have a problem and not close your eyes to it, or you will never get the help you need.

So again, our oneness was broken.

Just to be clear, all this time, I looked at my husband as the love of my life and soul mate. As I said before, the first ten years of our remarriage was great! During that time, he repented and had water submersion—baptism at Calvary Temple in Allentown, Pennsylvania. When he stopped going to church, he fell back into his addiction. It was about the same time I had a hysterectomy, and he never *knew* (had sex with) me after that time. He thought that because of the hysterectomy I was not a complete woman any longer. I am not writing this to make my husband look bad. However, you need the whole story. He just left addiction to sex take control of his life.

He was not just a good man—he was an amazing man. He would help anyone who would ask him for help and was well liked by his peers. He was supportive to me with a lot of my business meetings I had to conduct. He always looked for things to do for me that he knew would please me or which I asked him to do for me. He was always around when not at work—mowing, since we had a lot of land, or keeping things organized. TV was not one of the things he did a lot of. He was a good provider and great with the kids and grandkids. Face it. He had his moments when he was a man!

The grandsons look up to him because he was always there to help them no matter what was needed. Whatever he was working on was never as important as what they needed him to do. Because the grandkids lived close by, he was there to help the boys with learning how to use a hammer, fix their bikes, and always ready to give them a ride to practice or a game. They even wrote on a school assignment that he was their hero. I wrote my husband's eulogy, and I shared a Bible scripture that I thought he would want to pass on to each of the grandchildren. The one grandson even had the scripture he was given tattooed over his heart. It was of a tractor with the grass flying out because my husband was always mowing. The scripture was written as the flying grass.

For the two granddaughters, he was the only father figure they knew since their dad left when their mother was pregnant with the second girl. He was always there to pick up the girls at the babysitter after work or to babysit them. And the same with them if they got sick at school—he would pick them up or if they needed a ride to practice or a game. The other granddaughter was the youngest, and he loved teasing her. As soon as she walked in the door, he would say, "Go home." She was small, and at first, she thought he meant it, but he really didn't. He was just teasing her.

The reasons I stayed beside him was because I took a vow—"until death do us part"—and I took it seriously.

I learned a lot from being divorced. I realized that I let my heart rule, not my head. I did not thoroughly think and pray it out. We were soul mates. Would he have wanted to come back and get remarried if he, in his own way, did not love me? God put us together for a reason. During the whole time, I always loved him and would not do anything to hurt him.

Here are the reasons why I stayed.

1. I knew the damage a divorce could do to the family structure and how it effects the kids because we were divorced once already.
2. Even though his addiction hurt me, I noticed no effect on the rest of the family. I knew it was an addiction and he needed help when he was ready. He needed to come to the point that he wanted help. Would you abandon your spouse if they were a drug addict, alcoholic, glutton, or have another addiction?
3. I had lupus, and there was no insurance provided by my business, so I relied upon his insurance to cover me.
4. There was no resentment toward him, nor did I argue about it. He knew I was not going to make an issue about it. I just let him know I knew what he was doing was wrong, and I was here to support him and help him when he was ready because that's a wife's job, they are the helper.

I appreciate all he did to ensure that I was financially okay after his death. He hardly said he loved me, but because he stayed even with his addiction, I always believed he cared. Would he have been so supportive of me when I went to school and with my business if he did not care for me? One thing I know without a doubt is that he loved his kids and grandkids. He was a super dad and a super granddad.

Life as a family unit changed once the kids got older. They went on their own and had their own lives, not realizing how much they left behind, as well as how much they have taken with them.

Barbara Solt, a friend of twenty-seven years, was frequently at my house. After my husband passed, I told her about the things I was dealing with. She said, "I would not have thought there was anything wrong. Everything seemed normal."

My father suddenly passed away while in the hospital. I cannot remember ever being that traumatized. This was the worst trauma of my life. I could not talk I was sobbing so heavily. My mother also had cancer, and I took care of her for six months until she passed on. Her passing was peaceful, and I did not feel like it was a traumatic occurrence at all.

My oldest daughter had colon and pancreatic cancer. This was a very traumatizing time for me since she stayed with me during recovery after her surgery. The joy is that she is six years cancer free!

Now this brings us up to the time when I found my husband when he passed away in his sleep. I said earlier that I had lupus. I caught a virus and went deaf in my left ear. Because of this, when I took my hearing aid out, I was literally deaf, so I did not hear my husband when he passed away in his sleep. I went to wake him to go to the doctor's appointment when I found him. He died at 1:00 a.m., and I tried to wake him at eight thirty. Needless to say, I, like the rest of you, was traumatized! *My next marital trauma.* I think it is mostly because of the death being unexpected! It was the farthest thing from my mind that day.

Next are my health traumas. First major surgery was in 1972 with partial rib removal and top part of my lung. I have a floating rib. I had lupus from 1986 until it turned into Sjogren's. In 2018, I fainted and my painter caught me before I fell on the floor. My health issues just got more complicated. I had thirteen biopsies and left adrenal gland removal because I had pheochromocytoma (very rare), open-heart back surgery, collapsed lung, chemo for twenty-four weeks (no cancer) for nodules that were growing in my lungs (amyloidosis). I was told that I would be on chemo monthly for the rest of my life. I had three monthly chemo treatments when the chemo was completely stopped. Very exciting. Joy!

At that time, they thought amyloidosis was in the heart also. My prognosis was not good and did not give me much hope.

I was looking at this diagnosis being very short-lived since it doesn't give you much hope! I was given a six-month life expectancy. Trauma big time! To be sure, they had the right diagnosis, they did six biopsies of the heart to see if there was amyloidosis in my heart and it was not in my heart, so no six-month death sentence. Extreme joy! The bottom-portion of my heart was not functioning, but I will be okay because they said it would heal itself in two months. Super joyous! The diagnosis was stress cardiomyopathy. Something I wrote about under widows in the second chapter. Never thinking when I wrote about this in chapter 2 that I would have this as a diagnosis. During these three years, I looked to God since my help comes from the Lord. During that time, I prayed a lot for wisdom and understanding. As you can see, He brought me through the three years with more confidence in Him than ever!

Make sure you include all traumas in your life, not only marital—be it deaths of a sibling or child, spouse, mother, or father. Also, you are at your weakest whenever there is a trauma. Be careful not to let your mourning from trauma turn into grief. You need to move on. The best example I can give you is about water. Water needs to keep moving or it becomes stagnant. The same principle works for us. We need to keep doing something or we will become stagnant.

How soon everyone forgets how many times they needed you. When this is the time, you need them even more. You know the 75 percent loss of support base I mentioned earlier? This is what I mean. Those who support you now are only 25 percent of what you had before.

Then you wonder why the widows, divorced, or victims of adultery are lonely. They have lost most of the people who meant most to them, only because they do not have the time. It just was not the person who died, divorced, or the adulterous person that you lost but pretty much of your support base.

Time is our most valued asset. What do you plan on doing with your time instead of being lonely and in an almost comatose state? Use it well!

The days of our lives are seventy years;
and if by reason of strength they are eighty

> *years, yet their boast is only in labor and sorrow; for it is soon cut off and we fly away.* (Psalm 90:10)

Reaching eighty is one of my goals I put before the Lord, and so far He has pulled me through a lot of things. We can do it!

> *Teach us to number our days aright, that we may gain a wise heart.* (Psalm 90:12 NIV)

These last pages sum up my life and the trauma's I have experienced.

Since you took out your pen and paper, sit back and look at what you wrote about and write how many traumas you have had. Take a long look at your life. See what sums up your life and get ready to begin a plan for where you want to go from here. It is your life—what are you going to do with it? Sitting and just saying, "I'm lonely," all the time is not going to make the change you want and need to stop your loneliness. You and only you can do something about it! Philippians 4:8 will help you be aware of what you are thinking so you can be cautious of your thoughts. There is nothing there about wallowing in your loneliness.

Before you know it, we start letting "stinking thinking" sneak in. You need to nip it in the bud. The next scripture will help you do just that. It would do you well to memorize this. This is also a song I sing.

> *Finally, brethren, whatsoever things are true, whatsoever things are honest, whatsoever things are just, think on these things. Whatsoever things are pure, whatsoever things are lovely, whatsoever things are of good report; think on these things. If there be any virtue, and if there be any praise, think on these things.* (Philippians 4:8)

Before going into the next chapter, I need to share how God put widows in my heart. It started with a scripture.

> *Pure undefiled religion before God and the Father, is this; to visit the orphan and widows in their distress and to remain unspotted from the world.* (James 1:27)

The things I did with widows, over the next three years after my husband died, was my outlet instead of just sitting and trying to figure out what to do next. This was how I could help in little ways—to make the lives of others a little better. Guess what? It was also helping me with a reason to get out and do something for others. Everyone's talents are different, so use your talents not only to help others but so you can move on to become a better you.

I know there is a lot I don't know. I am just sharing what I learned by observation and doing something. Because I made many wonderful friends that I would not have known if I didn't take that first step.

I like the saying, "Get up, get dressed, get going!" That is what we should think about every day. I know we are older with aches and pains, but it seems they fade into nothingness if your mind is set on doing good things to help others.

In plain words, you just need something to do. Talk to God and ask Him to help you to use your strength and talents to help in the direction you should go. What do you like doing? Find out who you can share them with. This is all up to you so you have a more staple satisfying life.

*In all your ways acknowledge Him, and
He shall direct your path.* (Proverbs 3:6)

God has a plan for your life. Your spouse did not define you. He was an extension of who you are. This isn't the end. This is your beginning.

Your job now is to find the plan and start working at it—doing a little something daily. I hope you include talking to God—prayer (first telecommunications)—and, hopefully, you find a good church and read your Bible daily (God talking to you!)!

All these things are important for you to move on to a better life!

I shared some very personal things about myself that I would otherwise never talk about. These are things I would not normally share with strangers. Personally I would pull chapter 5 from the book; however, it is necessary for others to also have a chance for healing. I pray God can use it to help someone move forward as I have, no matter what happened in your life.

Chapter 6

OUR DEFINING HOPE!

As I said before, although I thought this was just going to be about widows, as I went along, God just kept showing me other things. These needed to be addressed because it deals with the same pain and issues that face widows that I did not cover in any other part of the book. Therefore, I need to end with the same way I started—with the widows but their plight in mind.

We need direction for our lives, not just in what we should do but what does God require of us. When I started working with widows, I naturally fell in love with my assignment. Currently, I want to help others and the church to recognize again their role in the life of widows.

> *He has shown thee O man what is good; and what does the Lord require of you but to do justly, to love mercy, and to walk humbly with your God.* (Micah 6:8)

I'm not sure when, but one day, as I was reading my daily scripture, this verse really got my attention again and made me see that God wanted more involvement with the widows—as a family and church again.

> *Pure and undefiled religion before God and the Father is this: to visit the orphans and widows in their trouble, and to keep oneself unspotted from the world.* (James 1:27)

In some versions of the Bible, the word *trouble* is translated as "distress."

This is one powerful verse of a scripture! Not everyone is called to have this as a driving factor in their walk with Christ. However, if you have a widow in your circle of contacts, you need to be sure you take heed to that widow and her distress. This is directed at you individually, but it is also the direction God wants for the church as well.

James is an epistle that was written for direction to the twelve tribes. The book of James starts with, "Count it all joy!" Can you do this with the widows?

All throughout the Bible, God provided ways to take care of the widow. Of course they always included things He wanted us to do in conjunction with what He wanted the church to do. The widow was always considered vulnerable, and therefore, there were many times that you see where God set guidelines and instruction toward the widows. The lines to this go from the Old Testament right through the New Testament!

There was always the concern of the widows not having enough to eat and that their immediate needs would be taken care of. The widow's vulnerability was always addressed in some way throughout the Bible.

There are many incidents—eighty-one total, with fifty-five in the Old Testament and twenty-six in the New Testament. As usual, I always share some scripture verses, so we'll start in the beginning, which is the Old Testament.

> *And the Levite, because he has no portion nor inheritance with you, and the stranger and the fatherless and the widow who are within your gates, may come and eat and be satisfied, that the Lord your God may bless you in all the work of your hand which you do.* (Deuteronomy 14:29)

> *When you reap your harvest in your fields, and forget a sheaf in the field, you shall not go back to get it; it shall be for the stranger, the fatherless, and the widow, that the Lord your God may bless you in all the work of your hands. When you beat your olive trees, you shall not go over the boughs again; it shall be for the stranger. the fatherless and the widow. When you gather the grapes of your vineyard, you shall not glean it afterward; it shall be for the stranger, the fatherless and the widow.* (Deuteronomy 24:19–20)

This is showing them not to take everything at harvest but to let something there that the stranger, the fatherless, and the widow are able to have food for their table. Notice though that they had to harvest it for themselves. God always had us work and not just expect everything to be given to us.

Another area was how to treat the widow and the fatherless child.

> *You shall not afflict any widow or fatherless child. If you afflict them in any way and they cry at all to Me, I will surely hear their cry; and My wrath will become hot, and I will kill you with the sword; your wives shall be widows, and your children fatherless.* (Exodus 22:22–24)

> *A father of the fatherless, a defender of the widows, is God in his holy habitation.* (Psalm 68:5)

> *The Lord watches over the strangers; He relieves the fatherless and widow; but the way of the wicked He turns upside down.* (Psalm 146:9)

> *The Lord will destroy the house of the proud, but He will establish the boundary of the widow.* (Proverbs 15:25)

These were in the Old Testament. Now let's see what the New Testament has to say.

> *Honor widows who are really widow. But if any widow has children or grandchildren, let them first learn to show piety at home and to repay their parents; for this is good and acceptable before God. Now she who is really a widow and left alone, trusts in God and continues in supplications and prayers night and day.* (1 Timothy 5:3–5)

> *If any believing man or woman has widows, let them relieve them, and do not let the church be burdened, that it may relieve those who are really widows.* (1 Timothy 5:16)

How do the churches measure up on what the Scripture requires of them? Where are we at as a church today? How was it set up in the early church?

> *Now in those days, when the number of the disciples was multiplying, there arose a complaint against the Hebrews by the Hellenists, because their widows were neglected in the daily distribution. Then the twelve summoned the multitude of the disciples and said, "It is not desirable that we should leave the word of God and serve*

> *tables." Therefore, brethren seek out from among you seven men of good reputation, full of the Holy Spirit and wisdom whom we may appoint over this business, but we will give ourselves continually to prayer and to the ministry of the word." And the saying pleased the whole multitude. And they chose Stephen, a man full of faith and the Holy Spirit, and Philip, Prochorus, Nicanor, Timon, Parmenas, and Nicolas, a proselyte from Antioch, whom they set before the apostles; and when they had prayed, they laid hands on them.* (Acts 6:1–6)

> *Then the word of God spread, and the number of the disciples multiplies in Jerusalem, and a great many of the priests were obedient to the faith. And Stephen, full of faith and power, did great wonders and signs among the people.* (Acts 6:7–8)

This is the way God set up how the early church was to aid the widows. When did this structure for the widows end? This never ended! (I found no scriptures to show where it stopped.)

Is your church doing what God wants for the widows? Are they following the way things were set up in the early church? Because when Stephen took up this ministry, the Word of God spread and disciples were multiplied. If you want more disciples in your church, apply God's principles for growth by taking care of widows biblically.

SEVEN REASONS WHY YOUR CHURCH SHOULD HAVE A MINISTRY TO WIDOWS

This verse cannot be more compelling or clearer:

> *Religion that God our Father accepts as pure and faultless this: to look after orphans and widows in their distress and to keep oneself from being polluted by the world.* (James 1:27)

Massive volumes have been produced by scholars on the biblical importance of caring for orphans and widows. I am grateful that churches around the world have taken some steps to care for the orphans, though much more remains to be done.

But in North American churches, there are hardly any intentional church-wide ministries to widows. Millions are left to suffer and struggle in silence.

To care for widows through the biblical mandate should be a sufficient motive for our church to consider some of the widows who experience struggles. These seven facts should give you at least a glimpse on the need for ministries to widows in your church.

1. *The death of a spouse is the number one stressor in a person's life.* Too many survivors are not ready to

deal with the issues of widowhood (Holmes and Rahe Stress Scale).
2. *Over fourteen million people are widowed each year.* Of that number, seven million are women (US Bureau of Census 2020).
3. *Widowhood lasts for fourteen years on the average.* That is a significant portion of any person's life (US Bureau of Census).
4. *There are over 14.75 million widows in the United States today.* That is an average of forty widows for every church in the United States (AARP).
5. *Upon the death of a spouse, a widow loses 75 percent of her support base.* It is imperative for churches to stand in the gap (Widow's Hope).
6. *Widows have a 30 percent higher risk of death in the first six months after the death of their husband.* They truly die of a broken heart (University of Glasgow).
7. *The poverty rate among widows is three to four times higher than elderly, married women.* Financial needs among widows are often great (Social Security Administration).

Please do not walk away after reading this short excerpt without considering some kind of action in your church to care for widows. It is one of the clearest mandates of the Scripture. It is also one of the most neglected mandates of the Scripture.

There are one hundred three verses in Scripture that show God's heart for widows and His instruction.

Did you know that half of the widows who attended church with their husband will stop attending within a year? What a loss to the church and the widows, only because of neglect to do what God requires—loss in wisdom that the widows have and what they can add to the youth in the church and the support they give to the church family. The church, in their neglect of the widows, are not representing the true family of God. Because in the United States, there are forty widows for each church, and if they don't have a widow's ministry, they are losing out. The widows have so much to add to the family. Is it too much trouble to pay back to the widow the years of devotion they gave you, plus all the support they gave you all those years? The church family is following the steps of the widow's family of neglectfully not heeding the widows' needs. They are no better than their family because they let them to their own resources.

You see, by following the way things should be carried out by the church—in taking proper care of the widows—there was an increase in disciples and many wonders and signs happened. Plus, disciples were added daily as noted in Act 6:1–8.

Caring for the widows is of vital importance for the churches. The quality of care for its widows is a barometer of the spiritual health and maturity of the church. If a church neglects its widows, something is amiss. What does the church do for the widows? Do they visit with the newly widowed person and discuss what they can expect of the church? Do they do any follow-up to see if they need any help and what kind? They won't ask!

Many widows do not need the financial support of the church. But caring for widows is not merely about financial support. Widows need lots of support and help as they adjust to life without their spouse. This may be required for a few months—others longer.

Because today, the widows often have greater financial resources at hand than during biblical times, what they need is for the church to have a specific widow ministry that extends past those first few months. Offer widows gathering opportunities so they can have fellowship time with other widows.

You will always see a great blessing when you do what God requires of you. You can see this in action with the best example of this being from the Old Testament in the book of Ruth. It showcases the underlying love of a woman for her mother-in-law and God's greater love through His care for both widows, Ruth and Naomi. Ruth was a childless widow, and she should have gone back to her family when her husband died. She chose, however, to stay with her mother-in-law, Naomi, who also was childless because her sons died. Ruth stayed to help her out since she was also a widow. Naomi returned to Bethlehem and Ruth went with her. Naomi had a relative of her husband, a man of great wealth named Boaz. Ruth asked Naomi for permission to go to the field to glean heads of grain, and she was hoping to find favor with Boaz. Naomi approved and told her to go. This is the first time she listened to advice from her mother-in-law.

The courtship with Ruth and Boaz was very unique since Naomi instructed Ruth throughout the whole process on how to do everything the right way. Boaz wanted Ruth for his wife, but the oldest relative always has first option to have them as their wife. This relative was not interested in having Ruth for his wife. So he and Boaz agreed that Boaz would take Ruth for his wife. They married, and Ruth conceived and gave birth to a son. Ruth said to Naomi, "Blessed be that the Lord, who has not left you this day without a close relative; and may his name be famous in Israel!" Naomi was his nurse. They called him Obed. If you follow his genealogy, David is from this line. And Jesus came from the line of David. It's amazing how God works in our lives for the greater good for us. Then we can say with Job that we:

> *made the widow's heart to sing for joy!*
(Job 29:13)

About the Author

Barb Neff's favorite hobby is tending to her flower gardens. Being an advocate for feral cats for thirty-plus years is her passion. She thrives on challenges and is willing to use her talents where needed.

She always had a love for learning. This love extended to the Bible and the Lord God. Because of these loves, she attended school to become a pastor. After finishing a year of school, this door was closed.

She started her own business, selling Longaberger baskets, rising to National Sales Leader in the company, which is the highest position you could acquire. Her personal sales exceeded one million dollars.

Being the author of this book is her latest accomplishment. What is the next thing God has for her to do?

Barb Neff is a lifelong resident of Eastern Pennsylvania with a Pennsylvania Dutch heritage. Widowed, she has four grown children, nine grown grandchildren, and ten great-grandchildren.

CPSIA information can be obtained
at www.ICGtesting.com
Printed in the USA
LVHW041529200723
752763LV00002B/521